Routledge Revivals

Financial Reporting in India

First published in 1986, *Financial Reporting in India* provides a comprehensive review of Indian financial reporting and makes a comparison with the United Kingdom. The book compares and contrasts financial reporting practices in the United Kingdom and India by examining the influences on accounting practices in the two countries and by comparing the actual accounting practices and level of disclosure of information in financial reports. It concludes by providing information on the amount of influence exerted by the United Kingdom on Indian accounting practices. This book will be of interest to students and researchers of economics and Asian studies.

Financial Reporting in India

Claire Marston

Routledge
Taylor & Francis Group
ROUTLEDGE REVIVALS

First published in 1986
by Croom Helm Ltd

This edition first published in 2025 by Routledge
4 Park Square, Milton Park, Abingdon, Oxon, OX14 4RN

and by Routledge
605 Third Avenue, New York, NY 10017

Routledge is an imprint of the Taylor & Francis Group, an informa business

Publisher's Note
The publisher has gone to great lengths to ensure the quality of this reprint but points out that some imperfections in the original copies may be apparent.

Disclaimer
The publisher has made every effort to trace copyright holders and welcomes correspondence from those they have been unable to contact.

A Library of Congress record exists under LCCN: 86002659

ISBN: 978-1-041-02074-5 (hbk)
ISBN: 978-1-003-61765-5 (ebk)
ISBN: 978-1-041-02079-0 (pbk)

Book DOI 10.4324/9781003617655

Financial Reporting in India

Claire Marston

CROOM HELM
London • Sydney • Dover, New Hampshire

Croom Helm Ltd, Provident House, Burrell Row,
Beckenham, Kent BR3 1AT
Croom Helm Australia Pty Ltd, Suite 4, 6th Floor,
64-76 Kippax Street, Surry Hills, NSW 2010, Australia

British Library Cataloguing in Publication Data

Marston, Claire
Financial reporting in India. – (Croom
Helm international accounting series)
1. Accounting – India
I. Title
657'.0954 HF5616.I4

ISBN 0-7099-4611-2

Croom Helm, 51 Washington Street, Dover,
New Hampshire 03820, USA

Library of Congress Cataloging-in-Publication Data

Marston, Claire, 1953–
Financial reporting in India.

(Croom Helm international accounting series)
Bibliography: p.
Includes index.
1. Accounting–India. I. Title. II. Series.
HE5616.I4M37 1986 657'.0954 86-2659
ISBN 0-7099-4611-2

CONTENTS

Contents

TABLES

FIGURES

To Peter Rowe for all his help and encouragement.

ACKNOWLEDGEMENTS

I wish to acknowledge with thanks The Institute of Chartered Accountants of India for granting permission to reproduce extracts from their publications.

My thanks are also due to the Indian companies who sent copies of their annual reports and permitted reproduction of extracts from them in this book.

Finally I would like to thank The Institute of Chartered Accountants in England and Wales for allowing reproduction of material from "Financial Reporting 1982-3" and "Financial Reporting 1983-4".

Claire Marston

PREFACE

This book was originally written as a dissertation leading to the degree of Master of Accountancy in International Financial Management and Reporting at the University of Glasgow. I am indebted to Professor S.J. Gray for his help and advice during the writing of this work.

The intention here is to provide a comprehensive review of Indian financial reporting and make a comparison with the United Kingdom. The material is up to date as far as possible to September 1984.

Claire Marston
Newcastle

INTRODUCTION

The fact that differences exist in the practice of accounting between countries has long been recognised by professional and academic accountants. Professional firms of accountants have collected information about the accounting practices in many countries. An example of this is the Price Waterhouse International survey (1973, 1975, 1979). Academic research has also been carried out describing different countries' accounting practices. Studies comparing the financial reporting practices of specific countries can also be carried out. Such studies can address the question why the various differences arise and possibly form a basis for consideration of harmonisation of accounting practices. This study attempts to compare and contrast financial reporting practices in the United Kingdom and India; firstly, by examining the influences on accounting practices in the two countries and secondly, by comparing the actual accounting practices and the level of disclosure of information in financial reports.

The study of international accounting contains various sub-sections. Firstly, the development of international accounting standards, both world-wide and within country groupings can be considered. Secondly, studies of the accounting and reporting problems of multi-national enterprises can be carried out. Thirdly, studies in comparative accounting which describe and compare financial reporting practices in different countries can be made. Comparative studies are of importance as they enable a better understanding of the problems of harmonisation and accounting for multi-national enterprises to be reached.

Attempts have been made to classify different countries' accounting systems into groups. This can be done subjectively, see for example Mueller (1967) or statistically, see for example Nair and Frank (1980). A system of classification based on judgement allied with methods used in the natural sciences has been suggested by Nobes (1983) and Nobes and Matatko (1980). Attempts at classification together with a knowledge of the underlying reasons for accounting differences should provide insights into the problem of international accounting standard setting.

McComb (1979) considers that:

> We are entering upon a phase of the process of the internationalisation of accounting in which attention should be directed towards achieving an understanding of the reasons for the continuing existence of national differences in accounting principles and practices. In that context, emphasis should be upon investigation, analysis, and education rather than upon speeding the process of promulgating further international accounting standards ... The case for harmonising accounting principles and practices on an international level is stronger today than it ever has been. True accord can be achieved, however, only if there is mutual international understanding, both of corporate objectives and the rankings attached to them.

There is a danger that international harmonisation programmes will not be properly conceived and may adopt a 'least common denominator approach' which cannot be considered totally satisfactory.

In recent years descriptive literature which can be used for comparison and classification has been produced. The emphasis appears to have been on developed countries and more information about less developed countries is needed as it is these countries that are particularly concerned about the activities and financial reporting practices of multi-national enterprises. This study attempts to contribute to the comparative accounting literature by comparing a less developed country, India, with a developed one, the United Kingdom.

The approach adopted is as follows. The accounting environment in both countries is described and a comparison attempted. The extent to which differing influencing factors might give rise to variations in accounting practices is considered. The accounting practices in both countries are then described and compared. The level of disclosure of information in financial reports is then tested empirically. Finally some conclusions are drawn about the level of influence exerted by the United Kingdom on Indian accounting practices.

Chapter One

ENVIRONMENTAL INFLUENCES ON ACCOUNTANCY

GENERAL BACKGROUND

It is to be expected that environmental conditions in a country will affect the accounting practices that develop. This idea has been discussed and investigated by several writers. Zeff (1971) demonstrated that accounting principles development comes from interactions between theory, practice and social, economic and political influences.

Choi and Mueller (1978, pp. 23-28) provide a list of environmental circumstances likely to affect accounting development. These include type of economy involved, legal system, political system and social climate. Abu-Jbarah (1972, p. 98) grouped countries by dominant economic characteristics using cluster analysis. Eighty countries fell into eight clusters and India's group also included Ethiopia, Ghana, Nigeria, Pakistan, the Sudan and Tanzania. The United Kingdom fell into a group of developed European countries, Australia, Canada and Japan. Arpan and Radebaugh (1981, p. 43) consider that a host of environmental variables affect any nation's accounting system. Similarities in accounting are based on similarities in environmental and economic characteristics. They consider that there are generally more commonalities in accounting among the industrialised countries and among the lesser developed countries than between these two groups. In some less developed countries however accounting is similar to highly developed countries. In this study the similarity between accounting in the United Kingdom, a highly developed country and India, a less developed country, will be investigated. The environmental influences to be discussed in this study are the legal situation, taxation, the stock exchange, the profession and the universities. Some general background information on the economy, political and social environment is now presented prior to examination of the above influencing factors.

India has had trading links with Western Europe from the early sixteenth century. The British East India Company increased its influence until, by the middle of the nineteenth century, it controlled virtually the whole of the Indian sub-continent. In 1858 the East India Company was taken over by the British government and until independence was attained in 1947, most of India was administered directly by the United Kingdom. Accounting and financial reporting practices were therefore largely based on the United Kingdom model although developments since independence mean that significant differences have arisen.

India is a developing country with a 700 million population that is growing at a rate of around 2.2 per cent, so every year there are 15 million new mouths to feed (see Table 1.1). The vast majority of the population live in the countryside (see Table 1.2), levels of literacy are low and accounting has little impact. In contrast India is the fourteenth largest industrial nation in the world. Amongst the developing countries only China, Brazil and Mexico surpass India.

Table 1.1: Area, Population and Employment in 1982

	India	United Kingdom
Area (000s sq.km.)	3,290	244
Population (million)	700 (approx.)	54.7
Population Density (inhabitants per sq.km.)	213	224
Total Civilian Employment (million)	180.5*	23.2

*1979

Source: International Labour Office (ILO) and HMSO.

Table 1.2: Distribution of Economically Active Population by Industry

	India		United Kingdom	
	Number '000	%	Number '000	%
Agriculture, hunting forestry and fishing	130,058	72.1	661	2.5
Mining and quarrying	923	0.5	350	1.3
Manufacturing	17,069	9.5	7,473	28.5
Electricity, gas and water	535	0.3	350	1.3
Construction	2,219	1.2	1,653	6.3
Wholesale and retail trade, restaurants and hotels	8,831	4.9	4,181	15.9
Transport, storage and communication	4,403	2.4	1,528	5.8
Financing, insurance, real estate and business services	1,209	0.7	1,425	5.4
Community, social and personal services	15,238	8.4	6,929	26.3
Armed forces			327	1.2
Unemployed			1,450	5.5
	180,485	100.0	26,327	100.0

Source: International Labour Office Year Book of Labour Statistics 1979.

The United Kingdom is an industrialised, highly developed country. The population size and growth is not generally considered to be causing severe problems. The generally higher living standards in the United Kingdom compared with India are reflected in a greater life expectancy (see Table 1.3). India's economy has been growing relatively slowly whilst other developing countries such as South

Korea have been showing impressive growth records. The United Kingdom's economy has also, in common with other developed countries, been growing slowly in recent years (see Tables 1.4 and 1.5).

Table 1.3: Expectation of Life at Birth

	Date	Male	Female
India	1961-70	46.4	44.7
United Kingdom - England and Wales	1976-78	70.0	76.2

Source: United Nations Demographic Yearbook 1981.

Table 1.4: Average Annual Rate of Growth of GDP per capita at Constant Prices

	U.K.	E.E.C.	India	Korea
1975	2.3	3.6	1.2	6.7
1976	2.3	3.5	1.2	6.8
1977	2.3	3.5	1.3	7.0
1978	2.3	3.4	1.4	7.2
1979	2.2	3.3	1.4	7.2

Source: Yearbook of National Accounts Statistics 1980 United Nations.

India has its own multi-national companies although these are small compared with the giant US multi-nationals. India has been exporting management and financial skills to Third World countries and OPEC countries. Agriculture does remain the crucial sector in the Indian economy with over 40 per cent of the country's gross national product being derived from agriculture and related activities. Under-employment, unemployment and the flood of country dwellers to over-crowded cities are all typical problems of developing countries that India shares. The vast contrasts in Indian society can be found reflected in the accounting profession. Bose (1977) states that while standards of the elite compare favourably with those of the developed west, those on the lower and middle reaches can be atrociously bad.

The political and economic environment since

Table 1.5: Gross Domestic Product and Growth

India	Gross Domestic Product Billion Rupees	Gross Domestic Product at 1975 prices	Exchange Rate Rupees per Dollar period average	Population Millions
1975	741.6	741.6	8.376	600.76
1976	805.9	815.6	8.960	613.27
1977	902.1	856.6	8.739	625.82
1978	974.4	824.4	8.193	638.89
1979	1061.5	878.29	8.126	650.98
1980	1256.8	-	7.863	663.60
United Kingdom	Billions of Pounds	Gross Domestic Product at 1975 prices	U.S. Dollars per Pound period average	Population Millions
1975	104.91	104.91	2.2218	55.90
1976	124.66	108.73	1.8062	55.89
1977	143.91	110.11	1.7455	55.85
1978	164.92	113.76	1.9195	55.84
1979	192.34	115.30	2.1216	55.88
1980	225.19	113.25	2.3263	55.95

Source: International Monetary Fund. International Financial Statistics.

independence has affected developments in accounting and financial reporting. India has used five-year economic plans inspired by the USSR in an attempt to advance towards a socialist but non-communist economy. Soviet aid has been used to help create India's heavy industrial base in the public sector. The five-year plans aimed at turning India into an industrial power by establishing the heavy industrial base to be followed by a consumer goods industry. Various measures were introduced to restrict imports of manufactured goods and to attract foreign and local investment into import substituting industries. Until 1966 the policies were successful and rapid industrial expansion was achieved. In the period from 1966 to 1975 a severe slowdown in industrial growth was experienced. The annual increase in manufacturing output averaged 3.5 per cent, less than half that achieved in the previous 15 years and far below the 7 per cent average achieved by the developing countries in total. Factors causing this were severe droughts, foreign exchange difficulties, the failure to seize opportunities in the rapidly developing foreign markets, inflation and the war with Pakistan and China.

Since 1975 India's economy has been severely affected by the sharp oil price increases. The government adopted an export oriented strategy, protectionism was relaxed, import regulations were liberalised and a significant increase in manufactured exports was achieved. A licensing system was set up with the declared objective of growth with social justice. The system favoured small to medium sized businesses in that many items of production were reserved for this sector. Firms were subject to licensed capacity regulations which meant that the main domestic manufacturing companies were unable to grow to obtain economies of scale and hence become more competitive. According to Caplan (1983) the officials dealing with the issuing of licences were able to supplement their income by enabling companies to circumvent the regulations so the adverse effects of the licensing system were illegally evaded to a certain extent.

The government has played a major role in industry having invested 240 billion rupees in public sector companies since independence (Emery, 1983). Public sector industries include steel, petroleum, coal, engineering and consumer goods. The public sector accounts for roughly one-third of employment and gross output in the manufacturing sector. It appears that Indian industry has become inefficient and costly however the protection offered by the government controls have allowed it to remain profitable. In the recent past a policy of liberalisation has been pursued. Industry is to be allowed to expand capacity by one third, and the number of industries in which large and foreign owned companies are allowed to operate has been extended from 19 to 24. Government controls have also been eased. A 5.7 billion dollar borrowing facility from the International Monetary Fund is expected to help export orientated growth. The sixth five-year plan (1980-85) set a target of 5.2 per cent annual growth but this is unlikely to be achieved. The above outlined re-orientation towards an outward looking development strategy and a more liberal domestic economic environment indicates a change in political attitudes away from favouring the Soviet inspired planned economy to a western style market economy. The comparative importance of foreign trade in the UK and Indian economies is illustrated by the relative size of imports and exports (see Table 1.6). The distribution of trade by area (see Table 1.7) reveals that the USA is India's largest trading partner. The government's ambivalent attitude towards capitalism and private enterprise has had a direct effect on accounting and financial reporting in that company law requirements in relation to disclosure and audit have in some areas been extended far more widely than in the United Kingdom.

Table 1.6: Foreign Trade 1979*

	India	United Kingdom
Total imports as % of GDP	8.2	29.0
Total exports as % of GDP	6.9	29.2

*Fiscal year beginning 1 April

Source: Yearbook of National Accounts Statistics 1980, United Nations.

India has a parliamentary form of government based on universal adult suffrage. It is patterned on the British system. The central legislature consists of the President and two houses, the Rajya Sabha and the Lok Sabha. Members of the Lok Sabha are elected directly by the people, it is the more powerful house. The Rajya Sabha is the Indian

Table 1.7: Trade by Area - (U.S. Dollars)

India (1978)	Imports	% of Total	Exports	% of Total
World	7,561,553	100.0	6,190,049	100.0
E.E.C. (9)	2,168,672	28.7	1,572,914	25.4
U.K.	556,442	7.4	519,021	8.4
U.S.S.R.	242,417	3.2	279,058	4.5
U.S.A.	906,294	12.0	820,948	13.3
United Kingdom (1980)				
World	117,902,094	100.0	114,380,488	100.0
E.E.C. (9)	48,115,108	40.8	48,310,209	42.2
India	733,370	0.6	1,229,958	1.1
U.S.S.R.	1,825,118	1.5	1,058,945	0.9
U.S.A.	13,915,850	11.8	11,854,562	10.4

Source: 1980 Yearbook of International Trade Statistics. United Nations.

equivalent of the United Kingdom's House of Lords, election is indirect and all legislation must receive consent from the Rajya Sabha. The union executives consist of the President, Vice-President and Council of Ministers. The President appoints the Prime Minister who is designated as the leader of the majority party or the coalition of parties holding the majority of votes. Executive power vests in the Council of Ministers, headed by the Prime Minister. The Indian states have their own separate governments, and the state government system closely resembles that of the union.

The languages of India are many, the official language of the union is Hindi but English is widely used especially in commerce. For example, annual reports of companies are produced in English and until recently the examinations of the Institute of Chartered Accountants have been exclusively in English.

The main religion of India is Hinduism (82.7 per cent of the population) followed by Islam (11.2 per cent) with major religious communities of Christians, Sikhs, Buddhists, Jains and Parsees.

To summarise, it is clear that there are significant differences between India and the United Kingdom. India is a less developed country with an enormous rural population whereas the United Kingdom is industrialised and highly developed with international trade accounting for a much higher per centage of economic activity than in India. However the long period of colonial rule of India by the United Kingdom means that certain similarities between the two countries continue to exist despite the fact that India has been independent for over thirty years.

THE PUBLIC SECTOR, STATE ENTERPRISE AND GOVERNMENT ACCOUNTING

Nationalised industry is an important sector of the Indian economy. In the manufacturing sector approximately 30 per cent of industry is state owned. The largest public sector enterprise, the Indian Oil Corporation, had a turnover of 35.725 billion rupees in 1978-79 compared with the largest private group Tata, with a turnover of 13.68 billion rupees. Dr P. Chattopadhyay (1981, p. 410) writes that the accounting practices followed by government companies estabished under the Companies Act have fallen into the enterprise accounting pattern and so are basically the same as private industry accounting practices. Public enterprises are subject to a professional audit as required by the Companies Act and in addition, to audit by the Comptroller and Auditor-General of India with periodic studies and scrutinies by the parliamentary Committee on Public Undertakings. The similarity of public and private enterprise accounts is an advantage in that greater comparability between the two sectors is achieved but the objectives of public enterprises could possibly be served better by a separately developed enterprise accounting system. Governmental accounting was initially based on the British system and has since developed to meet the needs of the Indian situation. Training of higher level accounting personnel in the government is carried out by the Indian Audit and Accounts Service and there is no effective link with the two professional bodies. The education programme is based on the stewardship concept with a lesser emphasis on performance budgeting. Entrants to different all-India services learn about governmental systems of accounts and audit in areas such as overall finance, defence, railways, revenue and customs and excise. The Ministry of Finance consists of four main divisions, Revenue, Expenditure, Economic Affairs and Banks. The Indian system embodies the principle of uniformity of accounting for transactions of central and state governments.

This uniform pattern for classification of accounts has obvious advantages for central government's information needs. The system is under the control of an independent Comptroller and Auditor-General. This organisation compiles accounts of expenditure classified according to major heads of account and subdivisions thereof. The Audit Department monitors the progress of expenditure against the budgeted grant.

The budgeting system of the Indian Government is of great importance in view of the successive attempts to achieve planned economic development. K.L. Handa (1980) has outlined the changes that have occurred since Sir James Wilson introduced the first budget in the government of India in 1860. This was the start of a highly centralised system of government accounting. A review by P. Appleby in 1956 noted that matters of detail were being referred to central agencies for concurrence even though the decisions regarding budgetary allocations had already been made. This resulted in delays, frustration and the nullification of decisions made earlier at the highest levels. Delegation of responsibility has been introduced by various schemes from 1958 onwards although, according to Handa, delegatees have not always accepted their new responsibility.

Line-item budgeting was introduced by the British but a need for performance budgeting has arisen because of the planned development under successive five year plans. This has been gradually introduced since 1968 as a management tool correlating physical and financial aspects of performance. In 1974 the government introduced a revised accounting structure which attempts to serve the purposes of management as well as the requirements of financial control and accountability. The system is not designed to relate to cost centres so further improvement is possible to enable government accounting to become a more effective management tool.

In the United Kingdom nationalised industry also forms a major part of the economy although the current Conservative government has been attempting to privatise as much state owned enterprise as possible. Certain state industries are subject to the accounting and audit requirements of the Companies Acts whilst others are subject to their own regulations. Governmental accounting has recently been subject to intense scrutiny as part of the Conservative election pledge to reduce public expenditure. Local authorities and health authorities etc. are required to prepare accounts according to relevant legislation and the recently constituted Audit Commission has been charged with appointing auditors and improving value for money. Central government accounting has been subjected to the scrutiny of the Morpeth Commission which recommended improvements to the internal audit service. Accountants in the government sector have their own specialised qualification, that of the Institute of Public Finance and Accountancy although accountants with other qualifications are also employed.

In both the United Kingdom and India state owned companies incorporated under the provisions of the Companies Act produce accounts in the same way as privately owned companies. A detailed comparison of other types of government accounting is outside the scope of this study.

LESS DEVELOPED SECTORS

The study of accounting and financial reporting in India is not confined to those areas already discussed, where the situation is one of relative sophistication compared with some developing countries. The agricultural sector is of vital importance to the economy. The collection of accurate statistics by the government has been hampered in the past by the lack of a farm accounting system. Systematised accounts keeping has not been carried out by individual farmers to any significant extent although the few government run farming companies do have fairly sophisticated accounting systems. The government has devised alternative methods of obtaining information in the absence of farm accounts. Farmers have provided estimates based on memory rather than written records and so the information lacks reliability. According to Bose (1977) there is no movement amongst accountants to offer their skilled services in the aid of agricultural development. On the contrary, Indian accountants are seeking lucrative employment in the Middle East.

Governmental accounting at the village level is under scrutiny as the traditional "Panchayati" system of administration is currently being updated and revitalised. The Panchayats will receive money flows in the form of taxes, grants and other receipts. Expenditures will be incurred under different headings such as rural development, capital investment and administration. A fairly sensitive system of accounting will be needed in order to be responsive to government aims.

An important sector of the economy consists of village and small-scale industries, cottage industries and small traders. There is difficulty in bringing this sector to a standard format of accounting practice as it is widely scattered and difficult to identify. The Development Commissioner of small-scale industries has recently obtained information from a census. Simple systems of financial and cost and management accounting are required in order to improve information for government and to meet the needs of small entrepreneurs. The current situation is that accounts are prepared when government, banks and other institutions request them, prior to granting assistance. Entrepreneurs need accounting education to enable them to do some basic recording of transactions since professional services are too costly for individuals in this sector.

A clear contrast can be seen between the areas of accounting and auditing under the Companies Act and governmental accounting compared with accounting in the village based and agricultural sectors of the economy. At the higher level accounting and financial reporting practices compare favourably with those in the west, as a result of the strong UK influence complemented by Indian developments and improvements since independence. At the lower level accounting is in its infancy, has little impact on the vast majority of the population and the lack of accounting is hampering government efforts to develop the economy.

LEGAL ENVIRONMENT

The legal basis of accounting and auditing in India is the Companies Act, 1956. Previous Indian Companies Acts resembled British law but did contain sections relating to problems peculiar to India. In 1950 the government appointed a committee to review the existing company law and to consider what amendments should be made. The British Companies Act, 1948 was used as a model for many sections of the new Indian act. Many of the existing provisions of the Indian Companies (Amendment) Act of 1936 were retained. In addition certain provisions were adopted which were considered to be an advance on the British 1948 Act. Of particular note was the introduction of a standard balance sheet format and a schedule relating to the contents of the profit and loss accounts. The British did not introduce a standardised format for accounts until the requirements of the European Community's Fourth Directive were enacted in the 1981 Companies Act.

The 1956 Act has been amended several times to eliminate practical difficulties and ambiguities. Disclosure rules have been extended by two Notifications issued in October 1971 and October 1973.

Companies (Amendment) Acts in 1965 and 1969 introduced regulations relating to the maintenance of cost accounts and requirements for a cost audit in certain companies. This will be discussed later.

Every company is required to keep proper books of account with respect to all sums of money received and expended, all sales and purchases of goods and the assets and liabilities of the company. The Companies Act does not prescribe the form in which the books are to be kept. The government has prescribed that several classes of companies engaged in production, processing, manufacturing or mining activities keep detailed records of utilisation of materials and labour and other items of cost. This power is granted to the government by s. 209(i)(d) of the 1956 Act and was introduced by an amendment in 1965.

At every annual general meeting the directors must lay before the shareholders financial statements containing a balance sheet and profit and loss account. The auditor's report and the directors' report must accompany these statements. The shareholders and debenture holders must be sent a copy of the accounts at least twenty one days before the annual general meeting.

If a company has subsidiaries it must submit audited financial statements and directors' report for each subsidiary. A statement must be attached showing the holding company's interest in the subsidiary at the end of the subsidiary's financial year. The statement must also show the interest in profits and losses not dealt with in the holding company's accounts. In contrast with the British 1948 Act, the subsidiaries' year ends need not correspond with those of the holding company but there must not be more than six months' time lag. If there is a time lag the holding company's accounts must disclose details of any changes in the interest of the holding company. Details of any material changes in the fixed assets, investments and loans given or taken by the subsidiary must also be disclosed. The Indian Act does not allow consolidated accounts as an alternative to the form of group accounts prescribed. The British Act requires consolidated accounts or a presentation of the same or equivalent information in a form readily appreciable by the company's members.

The auditor of a company is required to report to the shareholders on every balance sheet and income statement laid before the company in general meeting stating whether:

1. In his opinion and to be best of his information and according to the explanations given to him, the accounts give the information required by the Act in the manner required and give a true and fair view
   (a) of the state of the company's affairs as at the end of its financial year; and

(b) of the profit or loss for its financial year.

2. He has obtained all the information and explanations which, to the best of his knowledge and belief were necessary for the purposes of the audit.
3. In his opinion, proper books of account as required by law have been kept by the company so far as appears from his examination of those books, and proper returns adequate for the purposes of his audit have been received from branches not visited by him.
4. The report on the accounts of any branch office audited by a person other than the company's auditor has been forwarded to him as required by the Act and how he has dealt with the same in preparing the auditor's report.
5. The company's balance sheet and profit and loss account dealt with by the report are in agreement with the books of account and returns.

The legal requirement in India is for a more extensive report than required in the United Kingdom. The British law requires the auditor to consider all the above matters but positive confirmation is not made in the report. An example of an Indian audit report can be seen in Figure 1.8.

The auditor's duties in India go further as a result of an order issued under the Companies Act entitled 'Manufacturing and Other Companies (Auditor's Report) Order 1975'. This is known as the social audit order and applies to companies engaged in any of the four following categories of activity:

1. Manufacturing, mining or processing.
2. Supplying and rendering services.
3. Trading.
4. The business of financing, investment, chit fund, nidhi or mutual benefit societies.

(A 'chit fund', 'nidhi' or 'mutual benefit' company is a type of savings club. Subscribers are entitled to a prize amount when their number is drawn by lot. Also included in the definition are companies whose principal business is accepting fixed deposits from its members and lending money to them.)

Figure 1.8

THE TATA IRON AND STEEL COMPANY LIMITED
Auditor's Report

TO THE MEMBERS OF THE TATA IRON AND STEEL COMPANY LIMITED

We have audited the attached balance sheet of THE TATA IRON AND STEEL COMPANY LIMITED, as at 31st March, 1983 and also the Profit and Loss Account of the Company for the year ended on that date, annexed thereto.
We report as follows:

(1) As required by the Manufacturing and other Companies (Auditor's Report) Order, 1975 issued by the Company Law Board in terms of Section 227(4A) of the Companies Act, 1956, we annex hereto a statement on the matters specified in paragraphs 4 and 5 of the said Order.

(2) Further to our comments in the Annexure referred to in paragraph (1) above:
   (a) we have obtained all the information and explanations which to the best of our knowledge and belief were necessary for the purposes of our audit;
   (b) in our opinion, proper books of account as required by law have been kept by the Company so far as appears from our examination of the books;
   (c) the Balance Sheet and Profit and Loss Account are in agreement with the books of account;
   (d) in our opinion and to the best of our information and according to the explanations given to us, the said accounts except for quantification of additional gratuity liability as stated in note 5, give the information required by the Companies Act, 1956 in the manner so required and, subject to notes 3 and 4 regarding provision for depreciation, note 5 regarding provision for gratuity and note 8 regarding the Bihar Land Reforms (Amendment) Act, 1972, give a true and fair view -
      (i) in the case of the Balance Sheet, of the state of affairs of the Company as at 31st March, 1983 and
      (ii) in the case of the Profit and Loss Account, of the profit of the Company for the year ended on that date.

For A.F. FERGUSON & CO.,
Chartered Accountants,
V.K. KALRA
Partner.

For S.B. BILLIMORIA & CO.,
Chartered Accountants,
Y.H. MALEGAM
Partner.

Bombay, 23rd June, 1983.

The requirements of the order depend on the category of company involved. In the case of a company in category 1 the auditor is required to give his opinion on the adequacy of accounting records for fixed assets, stocks, scrap and by-product sales, loans made and investments. He must confirm that management have physically verified fixed assets and stocks. The report should contain details of fixed asset revaluations. If there are any loans from connected companies the auditor must report on them if the terms appear prejudicial to the company. In respect of loans granted by the company the auditor needs to confirm that repayments are being made as stipulated. The report should confirm the adequacy of the internal control procedures and in the case of large companies whether there is an internal audit system commensurate with the size and nature of the business. If the company is required by law to keep cost records it must be confirmed that this has been done. Where a company accepts deposits from the public the auditor must confirm that the relevant legal requirements have been complied with. In the case of provident fund dues the report must confirm that they have been deposited with the appropriate authority.

The requirements of the order call for a lengthy report from the auditor dealing with the above matters. A comment is required on all matters irrespective of whether the report is positive or negative. When an auditor is unable to express any opinion, he has to indicate such a fact and further must give his reasons why he is unable to express an opinion. The United Kingdom auditor is not required to make a report of this kind.

In the forward to the 'Statement on the Manufacturing and other Companies (Auditor's Report) Order 1975', issued by the research committee of the Institute of Chartered Accountants of India, the President, B.R. Maheswari explains the rationale behind the Order. He states that the need for such an Order arose from the fact that auditing procedures and practices had outgrown the form of audit report currently in use. It was felt that improved standards of performance attained by the profession, needed to be reflected in a more comprehensive form of report, and for that reason the Order was promulgated by the government, in consultation with the Institute.

Only chartered accountants within the meaning of the Chartered Accountants Act of 1949 can qualify for appointment as auditors. The rules relating to auditor appointment are basically the same as in the United Kingdom. Shareholders appoint the auditors at each annual general meeting by means of a special resolution. In the case of companies 25 per cent of whose capital is held singly or jointly by government, a prescribed financial institution, government company, nationalised bank or insurance company a special resolution requiring 75 per cent of the votes is needed to appoint or reappoint the auditor.

Where a company is 51 per cent owned by state or central government the auditor is appointed or reappointed by the central government on the advice of the Comptroller and Auditor-General of India.

As in the United Kingdom an officer, or an employee of a company cannot be appointed auditor. A person who is a partner or in the employment of an officer or employee cannot become auditor. A body corporate cannot act as an auditor. In India the number of company audits that may be carried out by an auditor is limited by the Companies Act. The maximum is twenty companies per partner in the audit firm. No more than ten of the companies should have paid up share capital over Rs 2.5 million.

As mentioned above, an interesting legal development in India is the inclusion in the Companies Act of provisions relating to the maintenance of cost records. These records must be appropriate to the industry and suitable for audit. The government Department of Company Affairs has the power to direct which companies shall be subject to these requirements. Dr P. Chattopadhyay reports (1981, p. 426) that twenty-eight industries have been brought under the purview of maintenance of cost records and audit of cost accounts. The government has laid down formats for the cost records and the audit report. The cost auditor must be a qualified cost accountant although chartered accountants are temporarily allowed to perform this role until the government announces that sufficient cost accountants are available. The reports are not made public but are examined by the government Department of Company Affairs. The government is in a position to monitor cost trends in different industries. In a developing country like India the scarcity of basic resources is a major problem and the cost audit is a valuable technique in mitigating the problem. The surveillance of plant capacity utilisation, material usage, labour costs and overheads is aided by standardised recording. Cost audit reports have been used by the government in fixing the prices of various commodities and in initiating corrective action in industries or units.

It can be seen therefore that the legal basis of accounting in India is the Companies Act 1956 which was greatly influenced by British company law. However subsequent amendments to the Act have adapted legal requirements to the needs of the Indian environment. The Indian government has increased the auditor's duties significantly with the 'Manufacturing and other Companies (Auditor's Report) Order 1975' and with the requirements for certain companies to keep cost records and submit to a cost audit. The United Kingdom government has not enacted similar provisions. However, Companies Acts in 1967, 1976, 1980 and 1981 have increased the work of auditors in other respects.

TAXATION

In some countries the revenue laws have a direct influence on reported profits. An example would be the requirement that depreciation charged in the accounts corresponds to the depreciation allowed under the tax legislation. In both the United Kingdom and India taxation computations are essentially separate from financial reports, however an Indian company which uses the Income Tax Act depreciation rates is not legally required to disclose its accounting policy and this option is favoured by many companies.

The Indian Companies Act requires that a minimum amount of depreciation be provided before any dividend can be declared. This minimum can be computed by applying rates allowable for tax purposes to the book value of each depreciable asset or by reference to the number of years for which depreciation allowances are given for tax purposes before a specific residual value is reached. Indian tax depreciation rates are at present roughly in line with accounting depreciation rates whereas in the United Kindom tax depreciation rates are used to accelerate relief for capital expenditure.

The Indian tax laws do not prescribe any method for valuing stocks. Any method that accords with sound commercial accounting principles is accepted by the tax authorities. This includes the 'last-in, first-out' (LIFO) method of valuation, which in times of inflation will reduce taxable profits. In the United Kingdom the accounting standard does not permit LIFO, whereas the Indian accounting standard does. In the United States the use of LIFO in published accounts is required if advantage is to be taken of the subsequently lower profit for tax purposes.

In conclusion, revenue law in both India and the United Kingdom has less effect on accounting than in some other countries. The taxable profits are computed by carrying out adjustments to the accounting profits although the differences between the two figures will tend to be larger in the United Kingdom because of the system of capital allowances.

THE ACCOUNTANCY PROFESSION

The accountancy profession in India consists of two main bodies, the Institute of Chartered Accountants of India and the Institute of Cost and Works Accountants of India. Both of these bodies are recognised by the government. The Institute of Company Secretaries of India is another professional body, its members are generally employed as secretaries of companies.

In 1949 the Chartered Accountants Act gave the Institute of Chartered Accountants statutory authority to guide and regulate the work of chartered accountants in the country. No equivalent act exists in the United Kingdom. The Act deals with incorporation of the Institute, entry of names in the register, fellows and associates, certificates of practice, use of the title 'chartered accountant' and the constitution and running of the Council of the Institute. There are provisions relating to misconduct of members, regional councils, penalties and other miscellaneous matters. The Act requires an auditor to disclose his financial interest in a client company if it is substantial. However a substantial interest is not defined in the Act.

In 1979 there were 21,000 chartered accountants with about a third in public practice, and the rest working in industry with a small number working in the government sector. About 45,000 candidates sit the Institute examinations every year. The professional examinations are of a high standard. There is an entrance examination for those who have not achieved a pass mark of 50 per cent in the Bachelor of Commerce examination at university or college. The intermediate and final examinations can be followed by special courses in management accountancy and corporate management.

The core subjects studied are financial accounting, auditing and taxation. The needs of the environment are taken into account in the professional examination structure. To illustrate, national (macro) accounting is now studied for the final examination. The following is the stated objective of the course:

> Its study sharpens the understanding of economic affairs of a country and Chartered Accountants should be able to master it. National accounting should also include public finance within its scope e.g. understanding the concept of public accountability in India, and an outline of the duties, functions and powers of the Comptroller and Auditor-General (Enthoven 1977, p. 266).

The Institute of Chartered Accountants publishes books and pamphlets for the education and guidance of members. Included in these publications, a full list of which is given in Appendix A, are guidance notes on accounting treatment of certain items and on different types of audit engagement. Various research works have been carried out and published, these include a 'History of Accountancy Profession in India' and 'Precedents in Published Accounts' containing extracts from annual accounts of the leading companies in India.

In 1976 the Institute decided to adopt the International Accounting Standards Committee's (IASC) standard on valuation and disclosure of stock. Bose (1982) reports that members forced the Institute to back down as they felt that home-grown accounting standards would be more acceptable to feelings of national pride. It was decided to set up an Accounting Standards Board (ASB) to harmonise the diverse accounting policies and practices in use in India. The ASB was constituted on 21 April 1977 and soon issued a 'Preface to the Statements of Accounting Standards'. This stated that 'the main function of the ASB is to formulate standards so that such standards may be established by the Council of the Institute in India' (1). In formulating the standards the ASB is to take into consideration the applicable laws, customs, usages and the business environment. The Institute supports the IASC and so the ASB will give due consideration to international accounting standards and try to integrate them, as far as possible, in the light of the conditions and practices prevailing in India. The ASB is responsible for propagating the accounting standards and persuading the concerned parties to adopt them. There is no professional obligation for members of the Institute to comply with the standards as is the case in the United Kingdom.

The preface states that in carrying out the task of formulation of accounting standards the intention is to concentrate on basic matters, to confine them to essentials and not to make them so complex that they cannot be applied effectively and on a nationwide basis. In the years to come, it is to be expected that accounting standards will undergo revision and a greater degree of sophistication may then be appropriate.

The following broad procedure has been adopted for issuing accounting standards. Firstly the ASB determines the areas in which accounting standards need to be formulated. In preparing standards the ASB is assisted by study groups constituted to consider special subjects. In forming these groups provision is made for a wide participation by members of the Institute and others. A dialogue with representatives of government, public sector undertakings, industry and other organisations is held in order to ascertain their views. An exposure draft of the proposed standard is prepared and issued for comments by members of the Institute and public at large. The draft includes the following basic points:

1. A statement of the concepts and fundamental accounting principles relating to the standard.
2. Definitions of the terms used in the standard.
3. The manner in which the accounting principles have been applied for formulating the standards.
4. The presentation and disclosure requirements in complying with the standard.
5. Classes of enterprises to which the standard will apply.

When comments on the exposure draft have been taken into consideration the draft standard is finalised by the ASB and submitted to the Council of the Institute. The Council may decide to modify the final draft in consultation with the ASB. The accounting standard is then issued under the authority of the Council.

The preface to the statements of accounting standards goes on to state that it will be the duty of members of the Institute to ensure implementation of accounting standards in financial statements covered by their audit reports. Any deviations from the standards should be adequately disclosed in their reports so that users of statements may be aware of the deviations. However, in the initial years the standards are recommendatory in character and compliance will not be enforced until a general awareness of the need for compliance with the above disclosure requirements has arisen.

The accounting standards programme in India appears to be closely modelled on the United Kingdom system. The similarities between the actual contents of the standards will be considered in Chapters 2 and 3. A list of accounting standards and exposure drafts issued by the Indian ASB is given in Appendix B.

The Institute of Chartered Accountants of India publishes a monthly magazine, Chartered Accountant (India), which features ASB material, the international accounting standards, articles on accounting, law, tax and auditing and news items.

According to Bose (1977) the profession has not come under pressure from shareholder and investor groups and the basic impetus for change has come from the government. In the early 1970s the state was nationalising banking and insurance and it appeared that the accountancy profession might also be taken over. Subsequently the government introduced a bill providing for three-yearly rotation of all audits but this was not enacted due to representations made by the profession. In 1976 the Minister of State for Law, Justice and Company Affairs told the Council of the Institute, '..... while ... in certain fields of your activities and organisation government intervention is unavoidable, the government will not unnecessarily interfere in your autonomy'. The disciplinary autonomy of the profession is regulated more closely by the Indian government than in the United Kingdom. The Chartered Accountants Act, 1949 provides that there shall be a Disciplinary Committee constituted from amongst the elected members of the Council of the Institute and one government nominee Council member. The procedures in inquiries relating to misconduct of members and appeals are laid down. Professional misconduct is defined and penalties are quantified. In important cases the punishment must be confirmed by the High Court. B.S. Mehta (1980) reports that since 1949 about 300 cases have been referred by the Council to the Disciplinary Committee and in two-thirds of the cases the members were found guilty. Of the 164 cases referred by the Council to the High Court and already disposed by the Court, in all but eighteen cases the Court agreed with the Council's finding.

The Institute of Cost and Works Accountants was set up 25 years after the United Kingdom Institute of Cost and Works Accountants (now the Institute of Cost and Management Accountants) and became a statutory body in 1959. Eventually cost accountants will be the only professional accountants able to perform the cost audits required by the Companies Act, 1956. There were 5,000 members of this Institute in 1979. The Research and Publications Committee has published a number of studies which are listed in Appendix C. These relate mainly to management and cost accounting. The training of cost accountants consists of work experience and an entrance, intermediate and final examination. In addition to the basic examination the Institute has an advanced level examination covering management accountancy, advanced management techniques, industrial relations and personnel, marketing organisation and methods and economic planning and development. This last topic enables the professional accountant in India to relate to the developing country environment and comprises the following:

1. Definition of economic planning: objectives, limitations and essentials of planning; communistic versus democratic planning; imperative and indicative planning; planning in backward areas. Different aspects of economic development; economic consideration; financial aspects; sources of finance.
2. Economic planning and development in India: mixed economy; five-year plans and industrial developments; specific areas of economic and industrial development; small-scale and large-scale industries; nationalisation. Appraisal of achievements; deficit financing; inflation; taxation and public debt; financial institutions; problems of population explosion and economic growth; food problem and food policy; agricultural developments; tariff policy; foreign exchange control; foreign

> private investments; climate and policy of foreign investment; foreign trade policy (Enthoven 1977, p. 267).

From the above description of the accountancy profession in India it appears that it is in many respects similar to that in the United Kingdom. However, the Indian Government does seem to exercise greater control in some areas than is the case in the United Kingdom. The profession seems to be geared to the needs of the developed, more industrialised, sectors of the economy. Compared with other less developed countries India is advantageously placed with a sophisticated professional structure and a large number of qualified accountants. Indeed, Bose (1977) reports that Indian accountants seek lucrative employment in the Middle East. The needs of the less developed sectors of the economy are now being considered in the educational programmes of both Institutes.

THE STOCK EXCHANGE

The Indian stock exchanges started informally in the eighteenth century when dealings in the loan securities of the East India Company were carried out. Share quotations were published in newspapers of the time. In 1850 an Indian Companies Act introducing limited liability was introduced. This gave further encouragement to the joint stock enterprise. At the same time the United Kingdom Joint Stock Companies Acts of 1844 and 1855 introduced the right to incorporate by registration with limited liability. The American Civil War induced a boom in the Indian cotton industry and from 1860 to 1865 shares traded in Bombay rose dramatically in price. With the end of the war a dramatic crash caused the investing public to lose their respect for brokers. The subsquent police harassment of outdoor trading caused the brokers to gather together in premises in Dalal Street in 1874. In 1877 they formed the Native Stock and Share Brokers' Association which set out to promote and regulate the activities of brokers.

The cotton textile industry developed in Ahmedabad and an association of brokers was set up in 1894. Trade was carried on outdoors until 1918.

In Calcutta the shares of companies in the jute, tea, coal and mining industries of the east were traded. This market was disorganised with a series of 'booms' and 'busts' until a communal riot in May 1908 led to the formation of the Calcutta Stock Exchange Association in June 1908. In the 1920s stock exchanges were organised in Madras, Lahore, Kanpur, Nagpur and Delhi. Rival stock exchanges grew up in Bombay, Calcutta and Ahmedabad.

After 1918 the Bombay stock exchange went through several crises and the subsequent public disquiet led to the appointment of the Atley Enquiry Committee by the Government of Bombay in 1923. The government did not act on the recommendations of the Committee although the market accepted some of the minor points whilst ignoring the major criticisms. After another crash in 1925 the Government of Bombay offered a charter to the exchange in return for authority to control the rule making. The offer was not accepted and a Securities Control Act was passed by the government in 1925. The Act specified that a stock exchange deal must be made according to government approved rules or the contract would be void. This Act proved ineffective in regulating security trading.

The Wall Street Crash in 1929 led to a crash in Bombay and in 1936 the Morrison Committee was appointed in response to further public criticism of the Bombay stock market. It made several recommendations that would attempt to curb reckless speculation. The stock exchange implemented some of the recommendations but others required further legislation which was not carried through as the Congress Ministers resigned in 1939 when the Second World War broke out.

The war caused a boom in share prices which started in September 1945 when the success of the Allies had resulted in increased business activity throughout India. The boom burst in 1946 causing serious financial problems in Calcutta and Bombay.

In 1948 a departmental committee headed by Dr P.J. Thomas, Economic Adviser to the Ministry of Finance, reported on suitable legislation for the regulation of stock exchanges in India. No action was taken until the government prepared a draft bill for stock exchange regulation in 1951. This was subsequent to the introduction of the new Constitution of India in 1950. An expert committee chaired by A.D. Gorwala reported on the bill and suggested changes. Subsequently the Securities Contracts (Regulation) Act, 1956 was passed. The committee suggested the establishment of an independent Securities and Exchange Commission, however the government did not act on this idea.

Singhvi (1967, p. 159) considers that the reason for this was the expense of such a body together with a failure to realise the need for it.

The Act permits the functioning of recognised stock exchanges only. Recognition is granted to an exchange only if central government is satisfied that its rules and bye-laws conform to prescribed conditions that ensure fair dealings and protection of investors.

The statutory Securities Contracts (Regulation) Rules, 1957 promulgated under the Act formulated a code of standardised listing regulations to be observed by listed companies.

Stock exchanges in India have been affected by the government's Foreign Exchange Regulation Act, 1973 (FERA). Multi-national businesses operating in India in certain industries were required to reduce their equity stake in stages until control by Indians was achieved. This led to public share issues by so-called FERA companies, an increased number of stock exchange investors and a greater volume of transactions (Pandey, 1981).

One way in which stock exchanges can influence the accounting environment is by including accounts disclosure or measurement rules in the listing agreements operated. In the United Kingdom the stock exchange requires disclosure of certain information in addition to that required by the Companies Acts. The Indian stock exchanges do not require listed companies to disclose any more than the legally required minimum. Gupta (1972, p. 233) has argued that 'In India at the present juncture where the resources of the common man are to be mobilised for the planned economic development of the country, there is all the more need for company accounts to be prepared in an attractive manner providing maximum amount of information in an easy and readily intelligible form'. He suggests that Indian stock exchanges should require listed companies to disclose more information in the areas of fixed assets, turnover, associated companies, funds flow, directors' report and chairman's speech. The lack of action by Indian stock exchanges in this area can possibly be explained by the lack of investor group pressure, the additional expense and difficulty of enforcement and the feeling that legal disclosure requirements are sufficient to satisfy information needs.

A study has been carried out to test whether the Bombay stock market is weakly efficient. Sharma and Kennedy (1977) tested the applicability of the random walk hypothesis in a less developed country, namely India. They also compared the behaviour of the stock market with London and New York. Over the eleven year period from 1963 to 1973 they examined movements in three stock market indices, the Bombay Variable Dividend Industrial Share Index (BVDISI) consisting of 603 industrial stocks, the New York Standard and Poor's 425 Common Stock Index (S & P 425) and the London Financial Times - Actuaries 500 Stock Index (London FT - A). One hundred and thirty two monthly observations were made. Based on the statistical tests carried out it was concluded that stocks on the Bombay stock exchange did 'obey a random walk and are equivalent in this sense to the behaviour of stock prices in the markets of advanced industrialised countries examined ...'

To summarise, the Indian stock exchanges have a long history as do those in the United Kingdom. In both countries their activities have been subjected to periodic government scrutiny. The United Kingdom stock exchange is generally considered to be efficient at the weak and semi-strong level in that future prices cannot be predicted from observations of past prices and that all current information is reflected in the market price of a share. It might be expected that the stock exchanges in a less developed country would be more likely to exhibit inefficiencies although it appears that the Bombay stock exchange is probably efficient at the weak level.

The influence of the stock exchange on financial reporting practices appears to be stronger in the United Kingdom than in India. In both countries however the stock exchanges do not enforce compliance with professional accounting standards as a listing requirement.

The Indian stock exchanges are not the only source of company finance. The main source of institutional finance are the financial institutions at the all-India level and the state level. These include the Industrial Development Bank of India, the Industrial Finance Corporation of India, the Industrial Credit and Investment Corporation of India, the Industrial Reconstruction Corporation of India, Life Insurance Corporation of India and Unit Trust of India. Emery (1983) reports that the development banking institutions had contributed over 40 billion rupees to the financing of private industrial investment during the 1970s.

The heavy reliance on financial institutions rather than the capital markets has been commented on critically for several years. M.Y. Khan (1978) carried out a study of the new issue market and finance for industry in India. The period of the study covered the years 1961 to 1973 and it revealed that the new issues market had a minor and declining role in the financing of corporate enterprises. Industrial entrepreneurs were relying heavily on the development banks. Most of the finance was provided in the form of term loans leading to a preponderance of debt in the financial structure of companies. The development banks derive most of their funds from the Reserve Bank of India or the government and Khan considers that the resulting divorce between the collection of savings and their allocation is an undesirable situation.

The above state of affairs appears to have arisen as a result of the heavy government investment in public sector industries. This has led to heavy taxes on private industry, high prices and costs and unattractive returns on investment. The capital markets declined and needed to be supported by the financial institutions (M. Ram and R. Patri, 1980). Table 1.9 compares the amount of finance raised on the capital market with that raised by the government.

Table 1.9: Capital Raised in India in 1967/68

	Rupees (Billion)
Response to government loans	
Amount of issue	
Central government loans	3.505
State government loans	1.253
Capital issues through prospectus	
Ordinary and preference shares	0.416
Debentures	0.174

Source: Report on Currency and Finance 1967-68, Reserve Bank of India and Economic Times April 7 1969.

A further source of finance for industry comes from the commercial banks. They do not subscribe to share capital and are subject to government regulations in that a maximum of 40 per cent of credit may be allocated to the commercial and business sectors. They are required to provide finance at concessionary rates to a variety of priority sector customers including exporters, farmers, small-scale industrialists and the self-employed. Foreign banks have been attracted to India by the absence of credit controls and the government have further encouraged them by allowing established foreign banks to open branches or representative offices. Emery (1983) considers that these measures should improve the flow of credit to industry.

ACADEMIC INFLUENCES

The universities and colleges of India have an important role in influencing accounting developments.

Entrants to the accountancy profession have in many cases completed the Bachelor of Commerce examinations. Commerce graduates with accountancy and auditing as special subjects and a mark of 50 per cent in their examinations are accepted as trainees by the Institute of Chartered Accountants (India). Other graduates are accepted if their marks are at least 60 per cent. The universities teach accounting practices and relevant legislation. Financial, cost and management accounting, auditing and taxation are all covered. Students may continue their studies at university by proceeding to the Master of Commerce course. Several universities offer advanced level accounting courses at this level. Accountancy is taught as a tool subject in management courses such as the Master in Business Administration (MBA), Diploma in Business Management (DBM) and Master in Business Management (MBM).

Indian universities are subject to severe problems such as high student/staff ratios and large-scale cheating in examinations. There are also problems in obtaining high quality staff. Professor S.K.R. Bhandari writes (1973) that the inadequacy of staff has led to poor standard commerce courses and relative stagnation in quality. Bose (1977) reports the following quotation from A. Sen, financial controller of the India Tobacco Company:

> Till sometime back, we were getting the dregs. Anybody can pass the Bachelor of Commerce Examination. At these examinations there is copying and examination questions

> are leaked. Also our universities are ill-equipped to turn out graduates of uniformly high calibre because of the sheer pressure of numbers.

Apart from providing entrants to the accountancy profession the universities are also engaged upon research. Chattopadhyay (1981, p. 419) considers that such research efforts have contributed substantially to the core of accounting knowledge in India. He reports that research into the problems of accounting in the less developed sectors of the economy has been lacking and in view of the massive government investment in this sector, more attention to this area is needed. At the time of writing he noted that the attention of researchers was being devoted to inflation accounting and liquidity management amongst other areas. One new accounting development stimulating the efforts of academic researchers was the publication by financial institutions of information about companies being assisted. This includes performance information, social cost-benefit analysis, value-added statements and information on investment employment relationships. Research has focused on further analysis of this new information.

Bodies concerned with accounting research include the Indian Council of Social Science Research (ICSSR) and the Indian Accounting Association (IAA). The ICSSR has organised research surveys in the areas of accounting and financial management. The IAA is a small body of academics who do limited research in accountancy.

The Indian situation can be compared with the United Kingdom where university and polytechnic degrees in accountancy are providing increasing numbers of entrants to the profession although non-relevant degrees are still accepted. Many students undergo professional courses at polytechnics and other colleges. The United Kingdom educational system, although suffering a period of financial cuts, does not experience the same problems as in India. The position of the United Kingdom as a wealthy western nation compared with India as a less developed country would account for the better facilities available. Accounting research is carried out in many universities and polytechnics and there are close links between the profession and the academic world.

To summarise, in both India and the United Kingdom higher education establishments provide training for prospective accountants and academic research is carried out.

The main influences on accounting appear to be the profession and the government although academic research and other activities are also important.

FURTHER INFLUENCES ON THE ACCOUNTING ENVIRONMENT

In addition to the matters which have been discussed in this Chapter, there are other factors which may influence the development of accounting practices and these must also be taken into account. In both the United Kingdom and India the presence of multinational companies may be an influence. International organisations such as the International Monetary Fund (IMF), the United Nations (UN), the Organisation for Economic Co-operation and Development (OECD) are involved in accounting matters and could be contributing to changes and developments.

The attitudes of management may be a relevant factor. The literature seems to suggest that both in India and the United Kingdom management are reluctant to disclose certain information because of fear of competitors obtaining an advantage. The practice of only disclosing the bare legal minimum of information seems to be more common in India than in the United Kingdom. Das Gupta (1977, p. 114) reports that most companies publish the minimum although a few progressive companies give much more information. Singhvi (1967, p. 166) concurs with this opinion and suggests that as many corporations are controlled by wealthy families a desire for personal financial privacy is a contributing factor. He also notes that Indian company management is reluctant to give out copies of annual reports to outsiders.

Any conclusions about similarities or differences between financial reporting in the United Kingdom and India must be considered in the light of current changes taking place in both countries. The United Kingdom practices have been, and will be, greatly affected by the European Community. Legislation has been passed harmonising accounting formats. Eventually a much greater control over financial reporting will be exercised. It is expected that India will not be directly influenced by European Community developments and thus greater differences between United Kingdom and

Indian accounting practices can be expected to develop.

India is a developing country and it may be more influenced in the future by accounting organisations oriented towards less developed countries. India is a member of the Confederation of Asian and Pacific Accountants (CAPA) but this group contains developed countries such as Australia and the USA along with Pakistan, Korea and other developing countries. The United Nations has been involved in the international accounting debate and India is one of the 32 nation members of the 'ad hoc intergovernmental working group of experts on international standards of accounting and reporting'. Developments at the United Nations are slow to materialise due to the difficulty of obtaining agreements in the face of widely opposing political views.

SUMMARY AND CONCLUSIONS

This study is concerned with describing financial reporting practices in India and making comparisons with the United Kingdom. This Chapter has attempted to compare the accounting environment in the United Kingdom and India. The environmental factors that have been examined are those that might be expected to influence financial reporting practices in both countries.

In comparing the general background of the two countries various historic, economic, political and cultural factors were noted. The long period of colonial rule of India by the United Kingdom leads one to expect that there will be considerable United Kingdom influence on accounting practices. India has, however, been independent for many years and is a developing country. One would therefore expect that divergences from the United Kingdom model will occur as financial reporting practices adapt to the needs of the changing environment.

Financial reporting practices in a particular country will be affected by legal requirements, including tax law, stock exchange regulations, professional organisations and academic discussions. These influencing factors have been considered and compared for the United Kingdom and India.

In the United Kingdom legal requirements have strongly influenced financial disclosure and dictated audit requirements. These legal requirements have been expanded considerably over the years in response to demands for greater accountability, comparability and more recently European Community laws. India has adopted very similar legal requirements which have been adapted to suit local requirements especially to provide the government with help in planning economic development. In both countries the taxation rules have had little impact on financial reporting practices, this is in contrast with the situation in many European countries where revenue law is a major consideration in determination of profit and accounts presentation.

The effect of capital markets on financial reporting practices has been stronger in the United Kingdom than in India. United Kingdom stock exchange regulations have required disclosure of information in excess of the legal minimum and publication of interim reports. The United Kingdom capital markets seem to be better developed than those in India. Although Indian stock exchanges have been in existence for a long time the literature seems to indicate that until recently they have been considered to be the province of the wealthy and a place where gambling occurs (Gupta, 1972).

The professional accountancy bodies in the United Kingdom have contributed significantly to the development of financial reporting practices especially since the commencement of the accounting standards setting programme. Disclosure of accounting policies has improved, methods of treating various items have been prescribed and so comparison between companies has been facilitated. In India the profesion has had an effect on financial reporting, however its standard setting procedures are lagging behind and seem imitative of the United Kingdom.

The environmental factors which have been studied and compared lead to the conclusion that financial reports in the United Kingdom and India will be in compliance with the legal requirements and oriented towards the needs of investors. In India, however, investor needs are possibly less well satisfied. Despite many differences there will be an underlying similarity resulting from the strong British influence before and even after independence.

(1) Reproduced by permission of The Institute of Chartered Accountants of India.

Chapter Two

INCOME MEASUREMENT AND ASSET VALUATION

INTRODUCTION

The environmental influences on accounting will affect the income measurement and asset valuation practices in a country. In both the United Kingdom and India, company law forms a basis for financial reporting practice. Accounts are required to show a true and fair view and certain rules are laid down regarding accounting practices to be followed. In both countries however, company law leaves a large amount of freedom in adoption of accounting policies, although the 1981 British Companies Act has reduced this freedom in some areas. The United Kingdom accounting standards programme attempts to narrow down the differences and professional accountants are required to follow its dictates. The Indian profession has followed a similar programme. However, at the moment the standards are recommendations only although eventually they will become obligatory.

Singhvi (1967, p. 171) reported that:

> The procedure of computing net profit differs in India from one company to another. It is also true in the United States but the degree to which net profit differs in the United States is less than it is in India ...

This comment appears to have some validity still but it is likely that further developments in company law and the accounting standards programme will tend to narrow down the differences.

This Chapter considers income measurement and asset valuation practices in India in comparison with the United Kingdom. This subject cannot be completely separated from the subject of disclosure of information which is dealt with in detail in the following Chapter.

A survey has been carried out by the author on the 1982 to 1983 accounts of thirty of the largest Indian companies. Details of the survey are given in Chapter 5. The aim of the survey was to assess the level of disclosure of information. The results of the survey will be referred to in this and the following Chapters.

The Research Committee of the Institute of Chartered Accountants of India has published 'Precedents in Published Accounts' (1981). This publication has the primary objective of highlighting the well established accounting practices being followed by the various companies in India and the preparation and presentation of financial statements. The survey covers the published accounts for 1979 of 202 Indian companies drawn from the private sector as well as the public sector. The results of this survey will also be referred to.

INVENTORIES

Indian company law currently requires the mode of valuation of stock to be stated and amounts in respect of raw materials, finished goods, stores and spares should be shown separately. Singhvi (1967) noted from his survey of 45 companies that no companies disclosed the method of inventory valuation. Das Gupta (1977) reported that not all companies surveyed by him disclosed the basis of valuation. By the time the Institute of Chartered Accountants of India carried out its survey of 202 companies in 1981, all but two disclosed the mode of valuation. Most companies specified the mode of valuation individually for each class of inventory but about one-third stated the mode on an overall basis. The great majority of companies used cost, lower of cost and market value, or lower of cost and net realisable value. Very few companies gave the meaning of cost or market valuation.

The Institute issued Accounting Standard 2, Valuation of Inventories (AS2) in June 1981. The standard states that subject to certain exceptions inventories should be valued at the lower of historical cost and net realisable value. The historical cost of inventories should normally be determined by using the 'FIFO', 'average cost' or 'LIFO' methods. The 'specific identification' method which attributes specific costs to identified goods that have been bought or manufactured and are segregated for a specific purpose may be used. The 'adjusted selling price' may be used where the inventory comprises items the individual costs of which are not readily ascertainable. The 'standard cost' method may be used if the results approximate consistently the results that would be obtained from FIFO, average cost or LIFO. The 'base stock' method may be used in exceptional circumstances only. The accounting policy adopted for valuation of inventories, including the cost formulae used, should be disclosed in the financial statements. If the base stock method is used the difference between the value at which it is carried and the value by applying the method at which stock in excess of the base stock is valued should be disclosed. Any change in accounting policy should be disclosed if it has a material effect. If possible the effect of the change should be quantified or the fact that the amount cannot be ascertained should be indicated.

The standard states that historical cost represents an appropriate combination of cost of purchase, cost of conversion and other costs incurred in the normal course of business, in bringing the inventories up to their present location and condition. Cost of conversion consists of costs which are specifically attributable to units of production and production overheads. The production overheads can be calculated according to the direct costing or absorption costing method and expenses which relate to general administration, finance, selling and distribution must be excluded. This requirement to include an element of overheads in such valuation is in agreement with SSAP9 in the United Kingdom.

In the author's survey, all companies revealed their stock valuation policies. Two examples are given below.

ASHOK LEYLAND LIMITED

Inventories

Inventories (other than stores valued at cost and machinery spares and tools charged off as incurred) are valued at lower of cost (excluding overheads) and estimated realisable value. Cost includes excise duty and customs duty when paid. Surplus/obsolete/slow moving inventories are adequately provided.

BHARAT EARTH MOVERS LIMITED

Inventory - Valuation

1. Raw materials, components and spare parts are valued at cost or estimates where costs are not available.
2. Work in progress is valued at cost. Cost represents materials, labour and appropriate overheads.
3. Finished stock is valued at actual/ estimated cost or realisable value.
4. Spares for resale are valued at cost less obsolescence by writing down the value over the years at a graduated scale depending on movement.

The situation in India compares with that in the United Kingdom in that inventory valuation policy is disclosed. The actual method of valuation is less standardised, possibly because of the lack of an obligatory accounting standard.

FIXED ASSETS AND DEPRECIATION

Indian company law requires a detailed disclosure of fixed assets in the accounts similar to that required in the United Kingdom. Fixed assets should be segregated under the following heads: goodwill, land, buildings, leaseholds, railway sidings, plant and machinery, furniture and fittings, development of property, patents, trade marks and design, livestock and vehicles. Under each head the original cost, additions and deductions during the year and the total depreciation written off or provided up to the end of the year must be clearly stated. In the case of revaluation of assets every balance sheet after the revaluation should show the revised figures and the date of the revaluation. Each balance sheet for five years subsequent to the reduction or revaluation should show the amount of the adjustment made. Depreciation should be provided on a consistent basis or if not, an appropriate note should be added to the accounts. Some Indian companies do revalue their fixed assets, although the Research Committee commented in 'Precedents in Published Accounts' that most stated fixed assets at historical cost. The legal requirements differ from those in the United Kingdom in that leaseholds are not classified into the categories long and short. Also the depreciation at the commencement of the period, for the period and on disposals need not be disclosed.

Das Gupta (1977, pp. 127-129) noted that not many companies disclosed depreciation provided during the year and on disposals. The survey of the Institute of Chartered Accountants of India noted that a large number of companies gave in some detail information about depreciation in excess of the basic legal requirement. One hundred and fifty-six out of 202 companies disclosed the opening balance of depreciation and the amount provided during the year. One hundred and forty-three companies also stated the provision for depreciation in respect of assets sold or discarded during the year. The author's survey found that all companies complied with the basic legal requirement. Additional information about opening depreciation and charge for the year was disclosed by 10 out of 30 companies, 9 disclosed depreciation on disposals.

In the United Kingdom there is a requirement to disclose capital expenditure contracted for but not provided and expenditure authorised by the board of directors but not contracted for. The Indian requirement is for a note stating the amount of capital commitments not provided for. Any advances can be deducted from this amount. All companies surveyed gave this information.

INFLATION ACCOUNTING

In common with the United Kingdom and many other countries in the world, India has been suffering from inflation in recent years and the problems of accounting for changing prices have been considered (see Table 2.1). Das Gupta (1977) reports that in 1950 the Chairman of Tata Iron and Steel Company asked the government to allow extra depreciation on fixed assets in order to meet increased replacement costs. He also states that at the time of writing a few companies were providing extra depreciation and creating a fixed assets replacement reserve. In 1976 a research study by Sen Gupta (1976) entitled 'Inflation Accounting in India' was published. In 1981 the research committee of the Institute of Chartered Accountants noted that 'some, though not many, companies presented supplementary inflation adjusted accounting statements: the method followed was the "Current Cost Accounts" method'(1). They give as an example the published accounts of The Projects and Equipment Corporation of India Limited. Their current cost accounts were prepared on the principles of the United Kingdom's Exposure Draft 18. In December 1982 the Research Committee published a guidance note 'Accounting for Changing Prices' which draws heavily on the work of the United Kingdom Accounting Standards Committee and recommends current cost accounting after outlining the method of the United Kingdom's Statement of Standard Accounting Practice Number 16. In the transitional phase it suggests that periodic fixed asset revaluation and LIFO inventory valuation would substantially reflect the impact of changing prices.

Table 2.1: Consumer Prices

% change over corresponding period of previous year calculated from indices

	1970	1971	1972	1973	1974	1975
United Kingdom	6.3	9.4	7.3	9.1	16.0	24.2
India	5.1	3.3	5.2	17.8	27.8	5.6
	1976	1977	1978	1979	1980	1981
United Kingdom	16.5	15.9	8.3	13.4	18.0	11.9
India	-7.8	8.5	2.5	6.3	11.5	13.0

Source: International Financial Statistics Yearbook 1982, International Monetary Fund.

None of the accounts surveyed by the author provided inflation accounts. An example of current cost accounts was found amongst the additional reports collected. Tata Chemicals Limited first prepared current cost accounts for its 1980 to 1981 annual report using SSAP16. This practice has been followed from 1981/2 and 1982/3.

The introduction to the most recent current cost accounts points out that the historical cost profit is converted to a loss by CCA adjustments. Management comments that:

> Current Cost Accounts will provide to shareholders and other readers a better insight into the deleterious effect of inflation both at the corporate and national level. Unless the results of an enterprise are evaluated after adjustment for distortions caused by

inflation, there is a danger both at the micro and macro levels that effective savings will be restricted, misallocation may be made of resources and direct cost-benefit relationships distorted.

GROUP ACCOUNTS

The Indian Companies (Amendment) Act of 1936 was the first legislation to require disclosure of information about subsidiary companies and annexation of their accounts with the holding company's accounts was made compulsory. The definition of holding company and subsidiary given in the Indian Companies Act, 1956 is basically the same as that in the United Kingdom legislation. A company is deemed to be a subsidiary if the other company controls the composition of its board of directors, or controls more than half the total voting power (where holders of preferences shares issued before the Act have the same voting rights as equity), or holds more than half in nominal value of its equity share capital, or finally if it is a subsidiary of any company which is that other's subsidiary.

The disclosure requirements in respect of subsidiary companies are extensive. Not only must the subsidiaries' accounts be annexed to the holding company accounts but in addition an extensive statement is required disclosing names of, interests in and total capital of subsidiaries. The profits since annexation and for the financial year dealt with in the accounts of the holding company, profits not dealt with in the accounts of the holding company, changes in the interests of the holding company between the ends of the financial years of the subsidiaries and the parent's year end and material changes in assets and liabilities of the subsidiaries between their year end and that of the parent company are all shown. In the profit and loss account of the holding company dividends received from subsidiaries, provisions for losses of subsidiaries and details of payments made to directors by the subsidiaries must be shown separately. The various types of inter-group balances must be shown separately in the balance sheet. The annexed subsidiary accounts must disclose the shareholdings of the holding company, its subsidiaries, the ultimate holding company and its subsidiaries. The identity of the ultimate holding company must be stated. Das Gupta (1977, pp. 152-60) provides a more exhaustive list of disclosure requirements along with a discussion of problems arising.

Consolidated accounts are not required by Indian law. The Bhabha Committee reported in 1952 on the provisions of the 1948 British Companies Act which contains the requirement for group accounts in the form of consolidated accounts or if the directors are of the opinion that it is better for the purpose the same information may be presented in a form readily acceptable for the company members. It considered that:

> the system of consolidated accounts is not likely to produce a correct and comprehensive picture of the financial position of the group. Apart from this fact, much more information can be obtained from the enclosure of the statutory accounts of the subsidiaries with the accounts of holding companies, as required by the present Act in this country.

Subsequently the preparation of consolidated accounts does not appear to have gained popularity in India. Das Gupta (1977, pp. 161-64) considers that group accounts disclose misleading information, that they are a 'fallacy to shareholders' and misguide creditors. He considers goodwill on consolidation to be a confusing item to the reader. He reports that only one company, Stanes and Company Limited, is known to him to be preparing consolidated accounts. Singhvi (1966, p. 171) however considers that the lack of consolidated accounts is a deficiency in Indian financial reporting as the inclusion of subsidiary accounts makes the annual report voluminous and it is difficult to determine the overall profitability of the firm.

The Institute has published International Accounting Standard Number 3 (IAS3) 'Consolidated Financial Statements' in the Chartered Accountant (India) magazine. In November 1982 an exposure draft 'Accounting treatment of reserves in amalgamations or mergers' was issued. Two situations are considered, an 'amalgamation in the nature of a merger' and an 'amalgamation in the nature of a purchase'.

In the case of a purchase of more than 50 percent of the voting shares a subsidiary is acquired and the question of treatment of reserves does not arise. In the case of a merger the identity of the various reserves of the transferor company are preserved and a capital reserve or goodwill balance may be created if the value of assets transferred does not equal the consideration plus reserves. If the amalgamation is in the nature of a purchase the identity of the reserves is not preserved unless the reserves were created by the transferor company pursuant to the requirements of the Income Tax Act. A balance on goodwill or capital reserve is created where the book value of the net assets of the transferor company is not equal to the consideration plus reserves required by the Income Tax Act. This exposure draft is significantly different from the United Kingdom ED31 'Accounting for acquisitions and mergers' issued in December 1982. The merger accounting method proposed entails creating an unrealised reserve on consolidation if applicable but any surplus value of the investment over shares received should be written off against reserves and not shown as goodwill.

There are no special rules or procedures for accounting for associated companies in India. The Companies Act does specify disclosure of investments in the capital of partnership firms. The names of the firms, all the partners, total capital and the share of each partner must be given.

In the survey carried out by the author only one company prepared consolidated accounts. Accounts of subsidiary companies were annexed to 17 out of 30 annual reports. The maximum number of subsidiary accounts attached was 21. Table 2.2 summarises the findings. This indicates that companies do not in general form themselves into very large groups in India.

Table 2.2: Attachment of Subsidiary Company Accounts to Annual Report

Number of subsidiary company accounts attached to annual report	Number of companies
0	14
1	6
2	2
3	3
4	1
5	2
8	1
21	1

FOREIGN CURRENCY ACCOUNTING

The Research Committee of the Institute of Chartered Accountants issued a 'Statement on Accounting for Foreign Currency Translation' in 1976. In the foreword it states that the Indian rupee, previously linked to the pound sterling, has its rate of exchange determined by the government on the basis of the exchange rate of a selected basket of foreign currencies. The introduction discusses the problem of floating currencies and the wide fluctuations that now occur. The following definitions are given: 'Permanent Change', a change in exchange rates which is in excess of 2.25 per cent of the rate at which the transaction or balance was last recorded or adjusted; 'Temporary Change', a change in exchange rates which is not in excess of 2.25 per cent of the rate at which the transaction or balance was last recorded or adjusted. The statement then proceeds to recommend the current/non-current method of translation (see Table 2.3). However where there has been a permanent change in exchange rates with the currency of the country in which a non-current asset is located, any diminution of the value in rupees may be written off if material. In the case of long-term liabilities where there has been a permanent change in the exchange rate the liability should be translated at the current rate. In considering the problems of accounting for translation differences the statement recommends that in the case of current assets and short-term liabilities, differences should be charged to profit and loss in the year they arise unless remittances are blocked where a gain should be transferred to a separate reserve account.

In the case of long-term liabilities when the funds arising have financed the purchase of assets still appearing in the balance sheet translation differences can be dealt with as follows:

1. Any profit should be transferred to a reserve account and a loss arising on subsequent translation can be debited to this reserve.
2. Any translation loss should be written off in the profit and loss account. If it is substantial the differences can be written off in instalments in proportion to the repayment of the liability in each of the subsequent years.

An alternative treatment is allowed in that the cost of the assets can be adjusted. This will cause problems with accumulated depreciation and the statements consider three possible methods and favours adjustment of the original asset cost and the recomputation of the accumulated depreciation.

Disclosure by way of a note is necessary. The following information is required:

1. A statement of translation policies including the exchange rates adopted for different items.
2. The aggregate amount of translation differences adjusted during the period indicating the net amount debited or credited to the profit and loss account and the net amount of differences dealt with in other fashion.

The Indian statement on accounting for foreign currency translation preceded a period of intense discussion in the United Kingdom. In 1977 Exposure Draft 21 proposed the closing rate or temporal method. In 1980 Exposure Draft 27 proposed the use of the closing rate method or the temporal method for certain types of subsidiary and became SSAP20 in 1983. It remains to be seen whether the Indian profession will be influenced by these changes. In the United Kingdom and the United States the current /non-current method is considered to be old fashioned, theoretically unsound and unsuitable for use with the large and frequent currency fluctuations encountered with free floats. The current/non-current method is, however, still in use in some countries and for example Flower (1985) reports that it is predominant in South Africa.

The Indian Institute's survey of the 1979 accounts of 202 companies showed that disclosure of foreign currency translation information is not widespread. Only 26 companies disclosed their accounting policy. The examples quoted in the survey comply broadly with the current/non-current method.

The author's survey found 9 out of 30 companies disclosing their accounting policy. Two examples are given below.

INDIAN AIRLINES

'The effect of revaluation of long-term liabilities due to currency fluctuations is adjusted at year end exchange rates, to exchange reserve account. Likewise, the effect of conversion of cash and bank balances in foreign bank accounts, deferred credit and advanced payments for purchase of aircraft as at the close of the year is also taken to the exchange reserve account. During the current year, the effect of revaluation of long-term liabilities resulted in a debit balance which has been shown as deferred exchange loss on assets side.'

ASHOK LEYLAND LIMITED

'Foreign currency conversion. Liabilities/assets in foreign currencies are reckoned in the accounts in the following manner:

1. Where the liabilities are covered by forward contracts, they are converted at the committed rates and any exchange difference arising on such conversion is reckoned in the revenue.
2. In other cases, they are converted at the rates the transactions are accounted in the books or the rates ruling at the year end whichever is higher in case of liabilities and whichever is lower in case of assets and any net overall exchange difference arising on such conversion is reckoned in the revenue.'

It should be noted that when an Indian company's foreign investment is a subsidiary company consolidation is not required. The subsidiary accounts are annexed to the financial report and can remain stated in the local currency. The Bombay Burmah Trading Corporation annexed the accounts of eight subsidiaries to its annual report for 1981/2. One set is in Indonesian rupees, one in Hong Kong dollars and two are in Malaysian dollars. A table at the end of the directors' report gives the opening and closing middle official rates for the year for eight currencies.

Table 2.3 summarises the recommended foreign currency translation method as set out in Statement on Accounting for Foreign Currency Translation issued by the Institute of Chartered Accountants of India (1982).

An Indian company needs to provide a certain amount of information about transactions in foreign

Table 2.3: Summary of Recommended Foreign Currency Translation Method

Balance Sheet	Rate
Current Assets	
- Non-monetary	C
- Monetary	C
Short-term liabilities	C
Non-current assets	H (2)
Long-term liabilities	H (2)
Revenue Account	
Revenue items	A
Opening stock	C (1)
Closing stock	C
Depreciation	H

C = current
H = historic
A = average
(1) = beginning of year
(2) = current rate if 'permanent change' has occurred

currencies to comply with company law. Exports and imports must be disclosed. Separate disclosure is required with reference to the value of imported raw materials, spare parts and components consumed during the accounting year. Any expenditures in foreign currency on account of royalty, know-how, professional consultation fees, interest and other matters must be disclosed. The amount remitted to non-resident shareholders on account of dividends paid in foreign currencies is a required disclosure. Foreign exchange earnings have to be disclosed in the following categories: (1) export of goods; (2) royalty, know-how, professional and consultation fees; (3) interest and dividends and (4) other income (indicating the nature thereof). The amounts listed should be stated in Indian rupees. In its 'Statement on the Amendments to Schedule VI to the Companies Act, 1956' the Institute states that the conversion should follow along the lines of generally accepted accounting principles as applied to the circumstances of the case.

The extent of disclosure of foreign currency transactions in Indian company accounts exceeds the United Kingdom requirements and the reason for this may lie in the fact that India is a less developed country with a government concerned to control the balance of payments and restrict imports and outflows of currency.

RESERVE ACCOUNTING

In the United Kingdom there has been a general trend to ensure that the results in the profit and loss account include those items that do not result from the normal trading activities of the company. Companies had been writing extraordinary items off to reserves in order to preserve an even growth in reported profits, other companies had been including these items in the profit for the year with a resulting lack of comparability between accounts. The accounting standard that was subsequently introduced required extraordinary items to be shown in the profit and loss account 'below the line', that is, after the figure for profits on ordinary activities after taxation. Any abnormal or exceptional items resulting from the ordinary activities of the company are disclosed 'above the line' if material. It is felt that this presentation will enable investors to assess the performance of the company and not be misled by the concealment of extraordinary items. The concept of stock market efficiency is relevant when considering the problem of disclosure of, and accounting for, extraordinary items. An efficient stock market will take account of all available information in setting share prices. If the extraordinary item is clearly disclosed it will not matter whether it is deducted in the profit and loss account or taken direct to reserves. Brealey and Myers (1981, pp. 268-70) discuss the subject of accounting changes and conclude that management cannot increase the market value of the firm by creative accounting.

The Institute of Chartered Accountants of India has also given attention to this matter and has issued an accounting standard 'Prior Period and Extraordinary Items and Changes in Accounting Policies' (AS5) (1982). Extraordinary items are defined as gains or losses which arise from events or transactions that are distinct from the ordinary activities of the business and which are both material and expected not to recur frequently or regularly. They include material adjustments necessitated by circumstances, which though related to previous periods are determined in the current period. The explanation to the standard mentions two approaches to the treatment of non-recurring items. One is to include them in the reported net profit or loss with a separate disclosure of the individual amounts. The other is to show such items in the statement of profit or loss after the determination of current net profit or loss. In either case, the objective is to indicate the effect of such items on the current profit or loss. Non-recurring items include extraordinary items, prior period items and items arising due to changes in accounting policies.

The standard requires that prior period items should be separately disclosed in the current statement of profit and loss together with their nature and amount in a manner that their impact on current profit or loss can be perceived. Extraordinary items of the enterprise during the period should be disclosed in the statement of profit and loss as part of net income. The nature and amount of each such item should be separately disclosed in a manner that their relative significance and effect on the current operating results of the period can be perceived. A change in an accounting policy should be made only if the adoption of a different accounting policy is required by statute or for compliance with an accounting standard or if it is considered that the change would result in a more appropriate preparation or presentation of the financial statements of an enterprise.

Any change in an accounting policy which has a material effect should be disclosed. The impact of, and the adjustments resulting from, such change, if material, should be shown in the financial statements. A change in an accounting estimate that has a material effect in the current period should be disclosed and quantified. Any change in an accounting estimate which is reasonably expected to have a material effect in later periods should also be disclosed.

The standard is similar to the United Kingdom standard in that all items are to be passed through the profit and loss account, however the inclusion of extraordinary items in net income contrasts with the United Kingdom method of showing these items below the line. The Indian standard makes no reference to the treatment of taxation on these items nor does it deal with adjustments arising out of revaluation of assets.

In May 1982 the Research Committee of the Institute of Chartered Accountants of India released a guidance note on 'Treatment of Reserve Created on Revaluation of Fixed Assets'. They consider that:

> The revaluation reserve is not available for payment of dividends. This view is also supported by the Companies (Declaration of Dividend out of Reserves) Rules, 1975. Similarly accumulated losses or arrears of depreciation should not be set off against revaluation reserve. However the revaluation reserve can be utilised for adjustment of the additional depreciation on the increased amount due to revaluation from year to year or on the retirement of the relevant fixed assets ... (1).

Having considered the legal position of accounting for the revaluation they make the following observations:

> The revaluation of fixed assets is normally done in order to bring into books the replacement cost of such assets. This is a healthy trend as it recognises the importance of retaining sufficient funds through additional depreciation in the business for replacement of fixed assets. As such, it will be prudent not to charge the additional depreciation against revaluation reserve, though this may result in reduction of distributable profits. This practice would also give a more realistic appraisal of the company's operations in an inflationary situation (1).

In the United Kingdom SSAP12 states that if assets are revalued the depreciation charge should be based on the revalued amount and in the year in which the revaluation is made the depreciation charges on the original and revalued amounts should be given. It would not therefore be acceptable to charge the extra depreciation against the revaluation reserve rather than against profits for the year. Nobes (1985) points out that the drafting of the standard is loose and a different interpretation does appear to permit charging the extra depreciation to a reserve or provision rather than the profit and loss account. Legally however the 1980 Companies Act states that where a fixed asset is revalued, written up in the balance sheet and subsequently depreciated, the depreciation charge relating to the revaluation surplus element will not be taken to reduce distributable profits. This may require companies to keep memorandum records of the accumulated depreciation on the revaluation element. Most companies would probably regard it as imprudent to distribute profits without deducting this additional depreciation.

The balance sheet treatment of reserves is governed by Schedule VI Part 1 of the Indian Companies Act. Reserves and surplus should be classified for balance sheet purposes as capital reserves, capital redemption reserve, share premium account, other reserves specifying the nature of each reserve and the amount, less debit balance in profit and loss account (if any), surplus, i.e. balance on the profit and loss account after providing for proposed allocations, proposed additions to reserves where it is necessary to obtain the sanction of shareholders and sinking funds. Additions to and deductions from all reserves should be clearly shown. This disclosure requirement is similar to that in the United Kingdom.

TAXATION ACCOUNTING

In the United Kingdom accounting for taxation is subject to the requirements of two accounting standards dealing with the problems of the imputation system and deferred taxation. The Indian corporate taxation system subjects companies to tax on their gross income and dividends distributed out of after-tax income are included in the taxable incomes of shareholders and taxed in their hands. Taxable profits are computed by adjusting the accounting profits for non-allowable expenses, certain amounts specifically allowed to be deducted, non-taxable items, weighted deductions with regard to certain specific expenses and some other items such as depreciation. In calculating business profits the cash or accruals or a hybrid method may be adopted provided it is followed consistently. Taxpayers are required to file statements estimating advance tax and to pay tax in respect of an accounting period in advance in three equal instalments. Taxes must be withheld at source from interest and dividends. There is no imputation system and the United Kingdom system of partial provision for deferred taxation in accounts has not been adopted in India.

The provision for taxation should be shown separately in the accounts and any advance tax is shown separately as a deduction from the provision for taxation or under the heading 'Loans and Advances' on the asset side of the balance sheet. The Institute recommends that if no provision for taxation is needed because of past losses a suitable note should be given to the accounts. Proposed dividends should be shown on the balance sheet before deduction of income tax. The profit and loss account should show the amount of charge for Indian income tax, other taxes, e.g. surtax, foreign taxes as reduced by double taxation relief, if any, available under Indian income tax law. Different taxes should be shown separately as far as practicable, e.g. income tax, surtax, agricultural income tax and interest tax.

The survey of the Institute of Chartered Accountants of India (1981) found that 192 out of 202 companies surveyed had a provision for taxation in their accounts. One hundred and thirteen showed the provision after deducting the amount paid as advance tax, 22 companies stated the gross amount and treated the amount of advance tax as an advance. In the remaining cases the treatment could not be ascertained. The author's survey of 30 companies found 29 which disclosed tax applicable to the current period in the profit and loss account.

INVESTMENTS

Indian company law requires a breakdown of investments between government or trust securities, investments in shares, debentures or bonds, investments in shares, debentures or bonds of subsidiary companies, investments in immovable properties and investments in the capital of partnership firms. The mode of valuation should be stated. The aggregate amount of quoted investments with the market value thereof should be stated. Das Gupta (1977, p. 129) reports that most companies disclose information as required by law but some companies do give additional information such as sales and purchases of investments during the year. The survey of the Institute of Chartered Accountants of India (1981) noted that the mode of valuation was clearly stated in general (see Table 2.4).

Table 2.4: Valuation of Investments

Mode of Valuation	Number of Companies
At cost	163
Below cost	1
Other	8
Not specified	20
	192
No investments	10
	202

All companies having quoted investments stated the market value. One hundred and eight just gave the total but 64 companies stated the market value of each investment individually. Figures for 87 of the companies showed a market value lower than cost but only 2 companies had made a provision for the fall in value of investments. There were no instances of investments having been written up although in 81 cases the market value exceeded the book value. The author's survey found that 26 out of 30 companies had quoted investments and they all gave the market value. An example from the accounts of Godfrey Phillips India Limited is given in Figure 2.5.

ACCOUNTING FOR CAPITAL BASED GRANTS

In June 1981 the Research Committee of the Institute of Chartered Accountants of India issued a 'Guidance note on accounting for capital based grants'. It listed the following principal methods of accounting for grants or subsidies:

1. The amount may be transferred to capital reserve which should be regarded as not distributable as dividend; or
2. The amount may be kept in a special reserve account and an appropriate amount

transferred annually to the profit and loss account with reference to the period specified in the scheme of grant or subsidy; or

3. The amount may be credited to the specific fixed asset for which the grant or subsidy was made available; or
4. The amount may be kept in a special reserve and a proportionate part transferred annually to the profit and loss account with reference to the life of the fixed asset for which the subsidy was made available; or
5. The amount may be credited to the profit and loss account of the year in which the undertaking becomes eligible to receive it or of the year in which the same is received; or
6. The amount may be kept in a special account to be transferred to the profit and loss account only when the conditions stipulated with the grant or subsidy have been fulfilled (1).

Figure 2.5

	1982 Rupees	1981 Rupees
SCHEDULE 5 - Investments (at cost)		
TRADE INVESTMENTS - QUOTED Molins of India Limited 3,500 (previous year 2,500) Equity Shares of Rs 10 each fully paid up (1,000 shares received as Bonus Shares during the year)	25,000	25,000
SUBSIDIARY COMPANY - UNQUOTED International Tobacco Company Limited 19,999 Equity Shares of Rs 100 each fully paid up	19,99,900	19,99,900
OTHER INVESTMENTS - UNQUOTED 35,300 Units of Rs 10 each of Unit Trust of India	4,44,985	4,44,985
GOVERNMENT SECURITIES - UNQUOTED	1,000	1,000
	24,70,885	24,70,885

(Market Value of Quoted Investments Rs 63,875; Previous Year Rs 53,125).

Method 1. is suggested as being applicable where the grant or subsidy is with reference to the total investment of an undertaking or by way of contribution towards the capital outlay of the undertaking and where such contribution has the characteristics similar to those of the promoters' contribution. Method 2. is considered appropriate where the grant is not related to specific fixed assets and where it is calculated by reference to the total capital expenditure or by reference to any other factor signifying the establishing of the undertaking as a whole and where it is considered as a compensation for the extra costs associated with the establishment of the undertaking. An example of this is a grant to aid establishment of an industry in a backward area. If the grant is given for the acquisition of a specific fixed asset method 3. may be used. This method is simple, it results in a lower depreciation charge and is in conformity with the income tax method of computing the cost of the asset. Method 4. is an alternative to method 3. that is considered acceptable. Methods 5. and 6. fail to match the revenue with the cost and are not recommended for use as normal accounting practice.

The guideline states that a disclosure should be made in the financial statements regarding the accounting policy adopted for the treatment of grant or subsidy.

The situation in the United Kingdom is covered by SSAP4 'The Accounting Treatment of Government Grants' which concentrates on grants in respect of particular capital assets. Methods corresponding to 3. and 4. are permitted but method 4. is considered preferable. If method 4. is used the deferred credit should be disclosed separately on the balance sheet.

ACCOUNTING FOR CONSTRUCTION CONTRACTS

In April 1983 the Indian Institute issued exposure draft 7 'Proposed Statement Accounting for Construction Contracts'. The exposure draft discusses the two methods of accounting for contracts known as the percentage of completion method and the completed contract method. The percentage of completion method involves recognition of revenue as the contract activity progresses based on the stage of completion reached. The completed contract method recognises revenue only when the contract is completed or substantially completed.

The standard proposes that in accounting for construction contracts in financial statements, either the percentage of completion method or the completed contract method may be used. The percentage of completion method can be used if the outcome of the contract can be readily estimated. Profit in the case of fixed price contracts normally should not be recognised unless the work on a contract has progressed to a reasonable extent. In the case of cost plus contracts, this degree of reliability would be provided only if costs attributable to the contract can be clearly identified; and costs other than those that are specifically reimbursable under the contract can be reliably estimated. While recognising the profit under percentage of completion method an appropriate allowance for future unforeseen factors should be made either on a specific or a percentage basis.

There should be disclosure in the financial statements of:

1. The amount of construction work in progress;
2. Progress payments received and advances and retentions on account of contracts included in construction work in progress; and
3. The amount receivable under cost plus contracts not included in construction work in progress.

If both the percentage of completion method and the completed contract method are simultaneously used by the contractor, the amount of contract work described in 1. above should be analysed to disclose separately the amounts attributable to contracts accounted for under each method.

The proposed standard allows either method of accounting for construction contracts. This can be contrasted with the situation in the United Kingdom where SSAP9 specifies that attributable profit should be recognised in the financial statements.

The 1981 survey of the Research Committee of the Institute of Chartered Accountants of India found only 3 companies out of 202 disclosing the treatment of expenditure during construction. The advent of the Indian accounting standard should increase the level of disclosure of the method of accounting for construction contracts.

SUMMARY

This Chapter has considered the topic of income measurement and asset valuation in Indian financial reporting. The relevant provisions of Indian company law and the pronouncements of the Institute of Chartered Accountants of India have been described. Comparisons have been made with the situation in the United Kingdom. The results of the author's survey and the survey of the Institute of Chartered Accountants of India (1981) have been incorporated into the discussion.

Some similarities have been found but there are significant differences. The main one is the presentation of group accounts. Consolidated accounts are not generally used in India whereas they are almost universal in the United Kingdom. India is lagging behind the United Kingdom in the development of inflation accounting although there is a clear United Kingdom infuence. In the case of foreign currency translation the influence of the United Kingdom does not appear strong but this is possibly due to the fact that foreign subsidiaries of Indian companies do not need to be consolidated.

The reasons for the differences noted above can possibly be attributed to the differing environments. In the case of group accounts, Indian companies do not tend to form themselves into large groups as in the United Kingdom. India is a less developed country and the resources needed to develop research in inflation accounting and to implement a national programme may not be available. India's currency is not freely floating nor is it freely convertible thus the problem of foreign currency translation is essentially different from that of the United Kingdom where the pound is floating and is a major internationally traded currency.

(1) Reproduced by permission of The Institute of Chartered Accountants of India.

Chapter Three

INFORMATION DISCLOSURE

INTRODUCTION

There have been several studies in which the level of disclosure of information in various countries has been compared using an index score (Singhvi and Desai, 1971, Buzby, 1974, Barrett, 1976). The construction of such an index entails selecting certain items of information that one might expect to find in a report and giving a suitable weighting to the various elements. A questionnaire may be sent to the relevant user groups or the subjective judgement of the researcher may be used in deciding on the composition of the index. Indices used in studies referred to have related primarily to investor needs. Accordingly information disclosed but not included in the index may result in erroneous conclusions being drawn about the level of information disclosure.

Singhvi (1967) has studied corporate disclosure in annual reports in India as compared with the United States. Using an index of disclosure consisting of 34 items he found that quality of disclosure was less good than in the United States at that time (1964 to 1965) (see Table 3.1). He concluded that:

> The disclosure of information in annual reports by the listed companies in India is less adequate and less investor oriented as compared to listed companies in the USA. Most of the Indian companies disclose in their annual reports the information which is required by the law, and the information which is required by the law falls short of what is desired by investors.

Table 3.1: Disclosure Scores for Listed Companies in India and the United States

Country	Mean score (out of 68)	Range of scores	Standard deviation	Sample size
United States	43.08	24-58	5.65	100
India	35.60	26-49	4.80	45

There have been significant developments in accounting in both India, the United States and the United Kingdom since 1965. More recent work on disclosure has been carried out by Das Gupta (1977) whose book surveys accounting practices without quantifying his observations. He based his work on annual reports of various companies ranging from 1962 to 1976 and reached the conclusion that:

> Most of the companies publish what is minimum and in some cases even violate the provisions of law but a few of the progressive companies like the Indian Tobacco Company Limited, Hindustan Lever Limited, Tata Group of Companies and so on, which have always been ahead of the law and have paved the way to progress for the other companies, give much more than this, and their efforts have been to provide the maximum information in an easily and readily intelligible form through schedules, charts and supplementary statements like the reports presented by companies in the USA, the UK and Australia.

In contrast with Das Gupta, the Research Committee of the Institute of Chartered Accountants of India (1981) comments in 'Precedents in Published Accounts':

> A significant feature of the published accounts was that much greater information than strictly required by law was being given. This has been discussed under the heads - statement of sources and application of funds, accounting policies, and information designed to make the accounts more intelligible (1).

DISCLOSURE OF ACCOUNTING POLICIES

In November 1979 the Accounting Standards Board issued Accounting Standard 1 (AS1) 'Disclosure of Accounting Policies'. In the introduction the Board comments that:

> In recent years a few enterprises in India have adopted the practice of including in their annual reports a separate statement of accounting policies followed in preparing and presenting the financial statements. In general, however, accounting policies are not at present regularly and fully disclosed in all financial statements. Many enterprises include in the Notes on the Accounts, descriptions of some of the significant accounting policies. But the nature and degree of disclosure vary considerably between the corporate and the non-corporate sectors and between units in the same sectcr (1).

The 1981 survey of 202 companies by the Research Committee noted that many companies 'disclosed their accounting policies even though the law does not require such disclosure except in a few specified cases and that too not in detail' (1). Table 3.2 summarises their findings. Thirty-eight of the surveyed companies disclosed accounting policies in a single statement, the remainder disclosed different policies at different places in the accounts.

The accounting standard explains the fundamental accounting assumptions of 'going concern', 'consistency' and 'accrual' and gives examples of areas in which differing accounting policies are encountered. The major considerations governing the selection and application of accounting policies are said to be 'prudence', 'substance over form' and 'materiality'. The standard states that all significant accounting policies adopted in the preparation and presentation of financial statements should be disclosed as part of the financial statements normally in one place. Any changes of accounting policies which are expected to have a material effect in later periods should be disclosed and quantified if possible. If a fundamental accounting assumption is not followed the fact should be disclosed.

The author's survey showed that many companies are still not following the recommended practice of stating accounting policies in one place. Only 9

Table 3.2: Disclosure of Accounting Policies

Accounting Policy	Number Disclosing (out of 202)
Basis of valuation of inventories	131
Methods of depreciation	38
Translation of foreign currency transactions	26
Treatment of retirement gratuity	14
Valuation of fixed assets	9
Treatment of research and development expenditure	6
Methods of insurance	4
Treatment of expenditure during construction	4

Source: Research Committee of the Institute of Chartered Accountants of India 'Precedents in Published Accounts' 1981.

out of 30 companies included a separate statement of accounting policies. This is in contrast with the current United Kingdom practice where such statements are almost universally provided. An example from the annual report of Bharat Earth Movers Limited is given below.

BHARAT EARTH MOVERS LIMITED

Accounting Policy

1. Fixed Assets - Capitalisation and Depreciation
   (i) Fixed assets are shown at cost. The land acquired free from Government of Karnataka at Kolar Gold Fields has not been valued. The expenditure on its development is, however, shown

against the cost of land.

(ii) Depreciation on fixed assets is calculated on straight line method; rate of depreciation is based on technical assessment of the estimated life of the assets.

(iii) In the case of different classes of assets in Township, rates of depreciation are based on Ministry of Finance OM No. BPE-1 (15)-ADV.F/69 dated 8.8.69.

(iv) Plant, machinery and equipment costing individually Rs 750/- and below are charged off to Revenue from the year 1977/78.

2. Inventory - Valuation

(i) Raw materials, components and spare parts are valued at cost or estimates where costs are not available.

(ii) Work in progress is valued at cost. Cost represents materials, labour and appropriate overheads.

(iii) Finished stock is valued at actual/ estimated cost or realisable value which ever is lower.

(iv) Spares for resale are valued at cost less obsolescence by writing down the value over the years at a graduated scale depending on movement.

3. Sales/other Income

(i) Sales set up for equipment is made when the equipment is unconditionally appropriated to the sale contracts after pre-despatch inspection by the specified authority.

(ii) Sales set up for spares is based on despatches against sale contracts.

(iii) Where sale prices are not established, sales are set up provisionally at prices likely to be realised.

(iv) 'Sales' exclude excise duty, sales tax and transit insurance but include anticipated price reduction due to contractual obligations like liquidated damages.

(v) Claims for cash assistance are accounted on accrual basis. From 1979 to 1980, claims for duty drawback on exports are accounted on cash basis.

(vi) Claims for service charges receivable from customers on their direct purchases from our collaborators and for price escalation on sales of EM Equipment are accounted on cash basis. In respect of Railcoaches and Trailers escalation claims are accounted on the basis of estimates.

(vii) Accounting for scrap is done at the time of sale/usage.

4. Gratuity
From the year 1979/80 the liability for gratuity is ascertained on actuarial principles and is being remitted into a separate fund.

5. Research and Development Expenses
The expenditure on Research and Development is charged to Profit and Loss Account in the year of incurrence. Expenditure on fixed assets relating to Research and Development are capitalised.

6. Rate of Exchange
Liability for deferred payments on imported equipment and components is reckoned with reference to the rate of exchange ruling on the date of availing the credit. The variation in the liability on account of fluctuations in the rate of exchange is accounted at the time of repayment.

7. Contractual Obligations
Warranty provisions for contractual obligations in respect of equipment sold to customers is set up on the basis of an annual assessment.

8. Others
(i) Inter-divisional transfers are valued at cost.

(ii) The cost of special tools and jigs is amortised over production based on technical assessment. The value is net as per books.

(iii) Hand tools are charged to expense at the time of issue.

(iv) Small value items are being charged to production at the point of purchase commencing from the accounts for 1976/77.

DEPRECIATION : DISCLOSURE OF ACCOUNTING POLICY

In November 1982 the Institute of Chartered Accountants of India issued an accounting standard 'Depreciation Accounting' (AS6). The standard is recommendatory in character in the initial years and is recommended for use by companies listed on a recognised stock exchange and other large commercial, industrial and business enterprises in the public and private sectors. The standard does not apply to forests, wasting assets, research and development expenditure, goodwill, livestock and land unless it has a limited useful life for the enterprise. The explanation to the standard notes that the statute governing an enterprise may provide the basis for computation of the depreciation. The Companies Act, 1956 provides that provision of depreciation, unless permission to the contrary is obtained from the central government, should either be based on the reducing balance method at the rates specified in the Income Tax Act (section 350) or on the corresponding straight-line depreciation rates which would write off 95 per cent of the original cost over the specified period (section 205(2)(b)). Where the management's estimate of the useful life of an asset is shorter than that envisaged under the provisions of the relevant statute, the depreciation provision is appropriately computed by applying a higher rate. If the management's estimate of the useful life of the asset is longer than that envisaged by the statute, a depreciation rate lower than that envisaged by the statute can be applied only in accordance with the requirements of the statute.

The accounting standard recommends that the depreciable amount of a depreciable asset should be allocated on a systematic basis to each accounting period during the useful life of the asset. The depreciation method selected should be applied consistently from period to period. A change from one method of providing depreciation to another should be made only if the adoption of the new method is required by statute or for compliance with an accounting standard or if it is considered that the change would result in a more appropriate preparation or presentation of the financial statements of the enterprise.

The useful life of a depreciable asset should be estimated after considering the factors such as expected physical wear and tear, obsolescence and legal or other limits on the use of the asset.

If the life of an asset is revised the

depreciation charge may be adjusted over the remaining life or the existing provision can be recomputed and adjustment made by means of an extraordinary item. Where the historical cost of a depreciable asset has undergone a change due to increase or decrease in long-term liability on account of exchange fluctuations, price adjustments, changes in duties or similar factors, the depreciation on the revised unamortised depreciable amount should be provided prospectively over the residual useful life of the asset.

Where the depreciable assets are revalued, the provision for depreciation should be based on the revalued amount and on the estimate of the remaining useful lives of such assets. If any depreciable asset is disposed of, discarded, demolished or destroyed, the net surplus or deficiency, if material, should be disclosed separately. The following information should be disclosed in the financial statements:

1. The historical cost or other amount substituted for historical cost of each class of depreciable assets.
2. Total depreciation for the period for each class of assets.
3. The related accumulated depreciation.

The following information should also be disclosed in the financial statements along with the disclosure of other accounting policies:

1. Depreciation methods used.
2. Depreciation rates or the useful lives of the assets, if they are different from the principal rates specified in the statute governing the enterprise.

The payment of management commission is based on a computation laid down in the Companies Act and disclosed in the notes of those companies to which it applies. Part of the calculation involves replacing the book depreciation figure by depreciation allowed under s. 350 of the Companies Act. This disclosure is undoubtedly of use to investors in cases where the method and rate of providing depreciation is not explicitly disclosed.

Das Gupta (1977, p. 138) had the following comment to make about depreciation:

> Depreciation policy is not uniform. Companies

> do not provide for depreciation at the same rate. In many cases the depreciation provision is not the same as allowed under Income Tax rules. In many cases, the amount of depreciation admissible under section 205 has not been disclosed, in which the shareholders are keenly interested. In view of the sizable difference between book depreciation under section 350, this information is very important.

The survey of the Research Committee of the Institute of Chartered Accountants of India (1981) found that only 38 out of 202 companies disclosed methods of depreciation.

The author's survey found that 15 out of 30 companies disclosed the depreciation method used. Two companies merely stated that depreciation has been calculated in accordance with s. 350 or 205(2)(b) of the Companies Act. (S. 205(2)(b) states that depreciation should be provided for such an amount as is arrived at by dividing 95 per cent of the original cost by the specified period as given by the Income Tax Act). Thirteen companies did not state the depreciation method, the implication being that they had used the method stated in s. 350 of the Companies Act which advocates the reducing balance method using rates in the Income Tax Act or the straight-line alternative given by s. 205(2)(b). Only one company disclosed depreciation life. Six companies made reference to the fact that depreciation life complied with the requirements of the Companies Act. One company just stated the depreciation life for leasehold land and stated that other assets were depreciated over their useful life. One company stated that rates of depreciation were not less than those required under s. 205(2)(b) of the Companies Act, 1956. The remaining 21 companies made no reference to depreciation lives, the implication being that rates complying with the Income Tax Act were used. An investor examining the accounts of an Indian company will in general need to consult the Companies Act and Income Tax Act to find out more information about the depreciation charge. As the effect of the accounting standard increases a greater level of disclosure should appear in the accounts.

The Indian situation in respect of disclosure of depreciation accounting policies is less satisfactory than that in the United Kingdom where SSAP12 and the 1981 Companies Act require disclosure of the accounting policy on depreciation. Apart from disclosing the method of calculation British companies generally disclose the rate or depreciation life of the different categories of assets.

SEGMENTAL REPORTING

The Indian legal requirements for segmental reporting consist of a requirement to show sales revenues by class of goods indicating the quantities of such sales for each class separately. The operating profit for each class of goods need not be shown. There is a requirement to state the value of exports but no other geographical analysis is needed. Segmental reporting of employee numbers is not required. These fairly modest disclosure requirements are exceeded by the British 1981 Companies Act and Stock Exchange requirements which require turnover and profit by line of business and geographical area to be shown. The average number of employees within each category of persons employed is required to be disclosed by the 1981 Companies Act. Categories must be determined by the directors having regard to the manner in which the company's activities are organised. The options appear to be a geographical or functional analysis or an analysis by product group.

Singhvi (1967, p. 169) noted from a survey of 45 companies that information on sales breakdown by customers or industry was not disclosed by any Indian company, while it was disclosed by 15 per cent of the listed companies in the United States. Information on sales breakdown by major product lines was disclosed by 13 per cent of the listed companies in India as compared with 26 per cent in the United States. This result was obtained prior to the introduction in 1973 of the Indian legal requirement for segmental reporting and the introduction in 1976 of the United States accounting standard FAS14 on disclosure of segment information.

The author's survey found that most companies complied with the basic legal requirements. No companies disclosed operating results by product line. Only two companies gave a geographical analysis of sales. The State Trading Corporation of India Limited gave an analysis of exports by commodity. The total for each commodity was broken down by country. A similar breakdown was given for imports. Pie-charts gave a summary by region of the detailed information. The Indian Farmers Fertilizer

Co-operative Limited gave details of sales of fertilizers by states in India. Information was in tonnes rather than rupees (see Figure 3.3).

It is interesting to note that the survey carried out by the Institute of Chartered Accountants of India (1981) makes no mention of segmental reporting. It appears that there is a lack of interest in this area of financial disclosure in India at present.

ACCOUNTING FOR CHANGES IN FINANCIAL POSITION

In June 1981 the Council of the Institute of Chartered Accountants of India issued accounting standard 3 (AS3) 'Changes in Financial Position'. The introduction comments that in many countries it is quite common to provide a statement of changes in financial position as part of the audited accounts. In India there is no legal requirement, however there is a growing practice to publish such statements. The objective of the standard is to encourage and strengthen this practice. The standard requires that a statement of changes in financial position should be published along with the annual accounts. Funds provided from or used in the operation of an enterprise should be shown separately in the statement of changes in financial position. Each enterprise should adopt the form of presentation for the statement of changes in financial position which is most informative in the circumstances. The appendix to the standard gives three illustrations of possible formats that may be used. None of these formats corresponds exactly to that given in the appendix to SSAP10 in the United Kingdom. The funds flow statement for a group is not discussed since consolidated group accounts are not generally prepared in India.

Singhvi (1967, p. 168) commented that only 6 per cent of 45 listed companies surveyed provided a statement of source and application of funds. Das Gupta (1977, pp. 172-76) writes that it is a recent tendency to include such statements in financial reports and that they appear in statement and diagrammatic form. The Research Committee of the Institute of Chartered Accountants of India found that very few of the 202 companies it surveyed in 1981 gave a statement of source and application of funds. The author's survey found that 12 out of 30 companies gave a statement and an example is given from the Report of The State Trading Corporation of India Limited (see Figure 3.4).

Figure 3.3
Extract from the Annual Report of State Trading Corporation of India Limited

COMPOSITION OF EXPORTS - 1982-83
- By Commodities/Countries
Item of value (FOB) of Rs 2 million and above

Commodity	Country	Rupees million
Coffee		
- Instant coffee	USSR	201.8
- Green coffee	USSR	690.1
	Japan	16.1
	USA	7.4
	Others	2.5
		917.9
Sugar	Indonesia	435.8
	China	174.5
	Sri Lanka	104.1
	USA	52.6
	Egypt	52.0
	Sudan	24.9
	Mali	2.7
	Lebanon	1.0
		847.6
Tobacco	USSR	383.0
	UK	91.7
	Switzerland	55.8
	China	41.5
	GDR	26.8
	Algeria	24.5
	Italy	15.9
	Japan	7.9
	Others	3.9
		651.0
Castor Oil	USSR	227.3
	Netherlands	127.6
	USA	62.5
	France	29.9
	Romania	14.7
	GDR	4.5
	Japan	2.6
	Australia	2.3
	Others	3.1
		474.5

Figure 3.3 (Cont'd)

Commodity	Country	Rupees million
GN Extraction	Poland	163.8
	GDR	150.8
	Czechoslovakia	79.7
	Malaysia	15.3
	South Korea	13.0
	USSR	3.8
	Bulgaria	3.0
	Romania	2.9
	Singapore	2.4
	Thailand	2.4
	Others	3.0
		440.1
Semi-processed leather	USSR	115.6
	Italy	107.3
	UK	90.6
	Japan	60.1
	Spain	15.7
	GDR	13.9
	France	13.3
	Czechoslovakia	7.9
	Poland	5.0
	Romania	3.9
	FRG	2.2
	Others	2.2
		437.7
Readymade garments	France	61.0
	USSR	60.8
	USA	58.1
	UK	52.7
	FRG	39.5
	Vietnam	22.9
	Italy	15.4
	Switzerland	8.3
	Australia	7.3
	Netherlands	6.0
	Canada	5.8
	Japan	4.3
	GDR	3.4
	Norway	3.3
	Sweden	3.0
	Denmark	2.7
	Others	9.2
		363.7

Figure 3.3 (cont'd)

Commodity	Country	Rupees million
Finished leather	FRG	57.9
	USSR	55.6
	USA	43.2
	UK	30.3
	Italy	25.7
	GDR	4.9
	France	4.6
	Netherlands	3.2
	Singapore	2.5
	Czechoslovakia	2.4
	Spain	2.3
	Hungary	2.2
	Others	6.1
		240.9
Jute goods	USA	73.8
	USSR	51.4
	UAR	35.1
	UK	17.0
	GDR	14.3
	Italy	10.1
	Ghana	7.9
	Czechoslovakia	6.3
	Iran	3.7
	Iraq	3.5
	Switzerland	2.9
	Canada	2.8
	Belgium	2.2
	Others	5.6
		236.6
Processed food/ fruits	USSR	147.1
	Saudi Arabia	17.8
	Kuwait	3.8
	USA	3.1
	UK	2.0
	Others	3.9
		177.7
Opium	USSR	69.5
	USA	32.2
	Japan	20.2
	Netherlands	18.2
	UK	12.7
	France	7.4
	Others	1.3

Figure 3.3 (cont'd)

Commodity	Country	Rupees million
Opium		
		161.5
Footwear	GDR	50.4
	USA	26.8
	UK	17.2
	FRG	9.6
	France	9.5
	Netherlands	6.7
	USSR	5.7
	Austria	4.5
	Denmark	3.8
	Others	8.1
		142.3
Shellac/seedlac	Singapore	23.2
	FRG	18.8
	USA	16.0
	UK	10.5
	Indonesia	9.6
	ARE	7.4
	Brazil	7.3
	USSR	5.8
	Malaysia	4.4
	Italy	2.0
	Others	23.2
		128.2
Cotton textiles	Switzerland	21.9
	Bangladesh	20.9
	USSR	15.2
	Italy	12.2
	France	10.4
	Czechoslovakia	10.1
	FRG	9.3
	UK	3.9
	USA	2.6
	Sweden	2.0
	Others	8.5
		117.0
Tea	Iran	53.3
	USSR	36.9
	Tunisia	6.1
	Poland	4.5
	Algeria	4.3

Figure 3.3 (cont'd)

Commodity	Country	Rupees million
Tea	UK	2.7
	Others	1.4
		109.2
Chemicals	USSR	91.3
	North Korea	2.5
	South Korea	2.5
	Others	5.6
		101.9
Footwear - components	GDR	82.6
	Denmark	9.8
	USSR	8.2
	Others	0.7
		101.3
Meat & marine products	Dubai	33.8
	Sri Lanka	18.1
	Japan	13.5
	Romania	10.7
	Kuwait	5.7
	Saudi Arabia	3.7
	Singapore	2.8
	Others	4.5
		92.8
Spices	Sri Lanka	41.7
	USSR	31.7
	Romania	5.1
	Poland	4.1
	Hungary	2.4
	Others	2.2
		87.2
Leather goods & garments	GDR	18.7
	FRG	8.5
	USA	7.5
	USSR	3.4
	France	2.9
	Sri Lanka	2.7
	UK	2.1
	Others	9.5
		55.3

Figure 3.3 (cont'd)

Commodity	Country	Rupees million
Rice	Kuwait	28.2
	Saudi Arabia	26.2
	Others	0.3
		54.7
Cosmetics & toiletries	USSR	51.1
	Others	0.5
		51.6
Salt	Bangladesh	23.3
	Nepal	7.8
	Malaysia	3.9
	Others	1.2
		36.2
Molasses	Netherlands	17.4
	UK	4.5
		21.9
Drugs & pharmaceuticals	Sri Lanka	9.2
	Nigeria	4.5
	Others	7.1
		20.8
Soyabean oil	Nepal	15.3
Timber & timber products	Qatar	6.6
	Oman	4.7
	UAE	2.3
	Others	0.9
		14.5
Coir products	USSR	5.2
	Denmark	3.0
	Others	6.1
		14.3
Lemon gross oil	USSR	9.7
	Others	2.8
		12.5
Henna powder	Algeria	8.5
	Turkey	1.3
		9.8

Figure 3.3 (cont'd)

Commodity	Country	Rupees million
Gramophone records	Hungary	5.4
	USSR	2.0
	Others	1.8
		9.2
Engineering goods	Iraq	2.9
	Others	3.5
		6.4
Tension bars	USA	4.2
	Others	2.0
		6.2
Plywood	USSR	3.1
	Others	3.0
		6.1
Vacuum flasks	USSR	4.1
	Others	1.4
		5.5
Sports goods	UK	2.0
	Others	1.5
		3.5
Spectacle frames	USSR	2.1
	Others	0.6
		2.7
Construction material	Australia	2.4

Figure 3.4
The State Trading Corporation of India Limited

FUNDS FLOW	(Rs Crores)*
*1 crore = 10 million	1982-83
SOURCE	
Funds from operations (profit before depreciation and tax)	62.98
Decrease in working capital	36.00
Total	98.98
APPLICATION	
Capital expenditure	2.60
Purchase of investments	37.50

Figure 3.4 (cont'd)

	(Rs Crores) 1982-83
APPLICATION	
Reduction in borrowings	16.98
Taxes	38.15
Dividend	3.75
Total	98.98
CHANGES IN WORKING CAPITAL	
CURRENT ASSETS	
Cash and bank balances	25.10
Short-term advances and interest accrued	15.54
Inventories	(80.76)
Sundry debtors	(23.46)
Total	(63.58)
CURRENT LIABILITIES	
Sundry creditors	(11.41)
Other liabilities	(9.49)
Provision for taxation	(7.47)
Provision for bonus	0.04
Dividend	0.75
Total	(27.58)
Decrease in working capital	(36.00)

FINANCIAL HISTORY REPORTING

The practice of providing historical financial statistics for a period of years is widespread in both the United Kingdom and India. Legal requirements dictate that comparative figures for the previous year should be given on the face of the accounts. Companies generally provide in addition information relating to a number of years. This may take the form of a table of figures or be presented graphically.

Singhvi (1976, p. 168) commented that the summary of important financial data for ten years or since inception of the company was disclosed by only 11 per cent of companies surveyed compared with 74 per cent of United States companies. Das Gupta (1977, p. 176) reported that most companies gave a statistical record ranging from 5 to 10 years. Contents differed from company to company as did the format. The survey of the Institute of Chartered Accountants of India noted that a large number of companies provided a summary of a number of years, often along with relevant ratios and statistics. Figures were given for a 5 or 10 year period. The author's survey found that 19 out of 30 companies gave information for 10 or more years. Seven gave details for 5 to 9 years and 2 provided 2 to 4 years' information.

The above results indicate that Indian companies have a fairly high level of disclosure in this area and that this has increased in recent years. An example from the annual report of Hindustan Ferodo Limited can be seen in Figure 3.5.

SIMPLIFIED ACCOUNTS AND FINANCIAL HIGHLIGHTS

The practice of giving simplified accounts and some details of financial highlights in addition to the statutorily required detailed accounts is widespread in both India and the United Kingdom. Das Gupta (1977, p. 166) noted that progressive companies were giving highlights statements under various titles including 'facts at a glance', 'the year in review' etc. In addition some companies were giving a summarised profit and loss account and balance sheet using simple language. In its survey of published accounts, the Research Committee of the Institute of Chartered Accountants of India (1981) reported that a large number of companies provided, as part of the annual reports a summary for a number of years often along with relevant ratios and statistics and that in addition some companies also gave a simplified summary of the current year's balance sheet and profit and loss account. The current survey found that the practice of providing simplified accounts and financial highlights continues to be widespread. An example from the annual report of The Tata Iron and Steel Company Limited is given in Figure 3.6.

REPORTING OF PRODUCTION CAPACITY AND CONSUMPTION OF RAW MATERIALS

The Indian government has introduced legislation to control the growth of industry. Large-scale production is subjected to a system of licensed capacity. Application must be made to the government before expansion is sanctioned. The aim of this policy is to encourage the growth of smaller businesses which are not subjected to the legislation. The Companies Act requires disclosure of licensed capacity and installed capacity. The

Figure 3.5
Hindustan Ferodo Limited

SUMMARISED BALANCE SHEETS

(Rs in lakhs)**

	1982	1981	1980	1979	1978	1977	1976	1975	1974	1973 9 months
Current assets	1271.7	865.7	1119.8	1019.1	1017.4	693.4	624.8	595.6	570.5	433.0
Current liabilities	389.3	242.1	308.7	343.3	278.7	218.2	216.6	229.6	172.1	175.0
Net current assets	882.4	623.6	811.1	675.8	738.7	475.2	408.2	366.0	398.4	258.0
Net fixed assets	178.0	173.2	180.8	173.1	160.5	160.9	167.5	182.6	185.7	191.4
TOTAL NET ASSETS	1060.4	796.8	991.9	848.9	899.2	636.1	575.7	548.6	584.1	449.4
Financed by -										
Equity capital	248.3	248.3	248.3	248.3	248.3	248.3	248.3	248.3	248.3	248.3
Reserves±	436.3	398.7	388.2	358.7	333.7	295.7	266.5	250.3	243.6	186.5
Borrowings	375.8	149.8	355.4	241.9	317.2	92.1	60.9	50.0	92.2	14.6
CAPITAL EMPLOYED	1060.4	796.8	991.9	848.9	899.2	636.1	575.7	548.6	584.1	449.4

S A L E S , P R O F I T S A N D D I V I D E N D S

(Rs in lakhs)

	1982	1981	1980	1979	1978	1977	1976	1975	1974	1973 9 months
Sales	2406.6	1306.0	1932.5	1848.1	1776.6	1576.5	1254.9	1035.8	1042.8	673.3
Profit before tax	211.5	75.2	245.5	235.4	293.2	275.9	198.9	141.5	203.0	119.1
Taxation	116.8	34.9	146.5	143.4	185.8	179.7	120.6	90.1	132.9	73.4
Profit after tax	94.7	40.3	99.0	92.0	107.4	96.2	78.3	51.4	70.1	45.7
Adjustments									5.6	
Retained profits	37.6	10.5	29.5	25.0	37.9	29.2	16.3	6.7	57.1	2.9
Dividends	57.1	29.8	69.5	67.0	69.5	67.0	62.0	44.7	18.6*	42.8
Dividends per fully paid share Rs	2.30	1.20	2.80	2.70	2.80	2.70	2.50	1.80	0.75*	1.725

* Restricted by the Companies (Temporary Restrictions on Dividend) Act, 1974.
± After adjusting dividends paid out of general reserve for the years 1973 to 1975.
** 1 lakh = 100,000

Figure 3.6

THE TATA IRON AND STEEL COMPANY LIMITED

Summarised Balance Sheet as at 31st March, 1983

		(Rupees crores) As at 31-3-1982
WHAT THE COMPANY OWNED:		
1 **Fixed Assets**		
Gross Block (original cost of land, buildings, plant etc.)	789.76	650.14
Less: Depreciation (loss caused by wear and tear)	369.45	346.09
Net Block	420.31	304.05
2 **Investments** in shares and securities	20.04	14.04
3 **Net Current Assets** - Excess of stocks and stores, customers' dues, advances and cash balances over current liabilities for supplies, services, taxes etc.	110.98	119.69
Total Assets (net)	551.33	437.78
WHAT THE COMPANY OWED:		
4 **Debentures**	50.50	50.60
5 **Other Borrowings**	264.59	183.14
Total Liabilities	315.09	233.74
THE COMPANY'S NET WORTH:		
6 **Shareholders' Equity**	236.24	204.04
(i.e. the excess of what the Company owned over what the Company owed) Represented by (i) Share Capital Rs 83.44 crores (Previous Year: Rs 83.44 crores) (ii) Reserves Rs 152.80 crores (Previous Year: Rs 120.60 crores)		
Total Capital **Employed**	551.33	437.78

Summarised Profit and Loss Account for the year 1982/83

		(Rupees crores) Previous Year
1 **Income** -		
Sale of our products	757.57	660.99
Interest, dividends, reimbursement of cost escalations for past years and charges for supplies and services rendered	40.59	43.70
Total Income	798.16	704.69
2 **Expenditure** -		
Raw materials, stores, wages and other expenses	686.52	581.44
Depreciation	28.42	27.21
Interest	38.35	18.39
Total Expenditure	753.29	627.04
3 **Profit before taxes**	44.87	77.65
4 **Taxes**	-	30.00
5 **Profit after taxes**	44.87	47.65
6 **Amount transferred from Development Rebate Reserve**	4.19	4.30
7 **Amount brought forward from previous year**	10.45	0.69
	59.51	52.64
8 **Appropriations** -		
Investment Allowance Reserve	18.50	12.50
Debenture Redemption Reserve	0.60	0.60
General Reserve	17.19	16.00
Proposed Dividends	13.09	13.09
	49.38	42.19
9 **Balance carried to Balance Sheet**	10.13	10.45

Figure 3.6 (cont'd)
SEVENTY-SIXTH ANNUAL REPORT 1982/83

Highlights

	1982-83	1981-82
	Million Tonnes	Million Tonnes
Saleable Steel - Production	1.621	1.606
Sales	1.463	1.415
	Rupees Crores	Rupees Crores
Gross revenue	**798.16**	704.69
Profit before taxes	**44.87**	77.65
Profit after taxes	**44.87**	47.65
Dividends	**13.09**	13.09
Retained earnings	**60.20**	61.77
Capital employed	**551.33**	437.78
Net worth	**236.24**	204.04
Borrowings	**315.09**	233.74
	Ratio	Ratio
Debt: Equity	**57:43**	53:47
	Rupees	Rupees
Net worth per Ordinary Share	**312.19**	267.48
Earnings per Ordinary Share	**61.12**	64.99
Dividend on Ordinary Share	**17.00**	17.00

licensed and installed capacity have to be stated separately in respect of each class of goods manufactured. The disclosure should be in accordance with the quantitative denominations mentioned in the licence. In addition to disclosing the licensed and installed capacity all manufacturing companies are required to disclose the quantities of their actual production. In its 'Statement on the amendments to Schedule VI to the Companies Act, 1956' the Institute comments the legal requirement is for quantitative information, however companies should link these details to financial information to make the disclosure more meaningful to shareholders.

There is a requirement to disclose raw materials consumed giving an item-wise break-up of quantities and values for all important basic raw materials. The value of imports of raw materials, components, spare parts and capital goods should also be disclosed.

FORECAST INFORMATION

In both the United Kingdom and India there is no legal requirement to give a profit forecast as part of the annual report. The directors' report in India should deal with the state of the company's affairs and this legal requirement is capable of wide interpretation. Das Gupta (1977, p. 142) noted that some directors' reports include, inter alia, plans for future development in operations or financial structure and forecast of future results. In his conclusions he considered that company law should be amended to require a note on future expansion, future financial requirements and future issues of bonus or rights shares. The survey of the Institute of Chartered Accountants of India (1981) note that a general, not quantified, statement about future expectations was quite common in the chairman's speech and that 104 of the 202 companies surveyed included information on future plans in the directors' report. The author's survey also contained examples of forecast information.

The chairman's report of The Tata Iron and Steel Company Limited contained prospective information under the headings 'the year's prospects', 'modernisation: cost and benefits' and 'looking ahead'. No firm profits forecasts were made although details of modernisation project costs were given.

The directors' report for Bharat Earth Movers Limited included a section on 'performance and prospects' which commented on plans for further growth with no attempt at quantifying them.

DISCLOSURE OF INFORMATION IN THE PROFIT AND LOSS ACCOUNT

In India and the United Kingdom, company law prescribes a certain amount of information relating to income and expenditure that must be disclosed on the face of the accounts or in a supplementary note. The 1981 Companies Act in the United Kingdom has recently extended the disclosure requirements which were previously fairly modest in certain respects. The following review of Indian disclosure requirements will show that they exceed United Kingdom requirements in the area of sales, consumption of raw materials and certain expenditure items. In the United Kingdom the additional requirements of the stock exchange increase disclosure for publicly quoted companies whereas Indian stock exchanges do not impose such requirements.

There is no prescribed format for the Indian profit and loss account. It should disclose the following items:

1. (a) The turnover, that is, the aggregate amount for which sales are effected by the company, giving the amount of sales in respect of each class of goods dealt with by the company and indicating the quantities of such sales.
   (b) Commission paid to sole selling agents.
   (c) Commission paid to other agents.
   (d) Brokerage and discounts on sales other than the usual trade discount.
2. In the case of manufacturing companies:
   (a) The value of raw materials consumed, giving item-wise break-up and indicating quantities thereof.
   (b) The opening and closing stock of goods produced giving break-up in respect of each class of goods and indicating the quantities thereof.
3. In the case of trading concerns:
   (a) The total purchases made and opening and closing stocks giving a break-up in respect of each class of goods traded in.
4. In the case of a concern rendering or supplying services:
   (a) The gross income derived from services rendered or supplied.
5. In the case of a company which falls under more than one of the categories mentioned

in 2, 3 and 4, it shall be sufficient compliance if the total amounts are shown in respect of the opening and closing stocks, purchases, sales and consumption of raw materials with value and quantitative break-up and the gross income from services rendered is shown.

6. In the case of other companies the gross income derived under different heads.
7. In the case of all concerns having works-in-progress, opening and closing figures of works completed.
8. The amount provided for depreciation, renewals or diminution in the value of fixed assets.
   If such provision is not made by means of a depreciation charge, the method adopted for making such provision. If no provision has been made, the fact shall be stated and the quantum of arrears of depreciation computed in accordance with s. 205(2) of the Act shall be disclosed by way of a note.
9. The amount of interest on the company's debentures and other fixed loans, i.e. loans for fixed periods stating separately the amount of interest, if any, paid or payable to the managing director, and the manager, if any.
10. The amount of charge for Indian income tax and other Indian taxation on profits. The amount of tax imposed elsewhere to the extent of the relief, if any, from Indian income tax and, where practicable, different taxes should be shown separately.
11. The amounts reserved for:
    (a) Repayment of share capital, and
    (b) Repayment of loans.
12. The aggregate, if material, of any amounts set aside or proposed to be set aside to reserves or withdrawn from reserves, but not including a provision made to meet any specific liability, contingency or commitment known to exist at the date at which the balance sheet is made up.
13. The aggregate, if material, of the amounts set aside to provisions made for meeting specific liabilities, contingencies or commitments or of the amounts withdrawn from such provisions, as no longer required.
14. Expenditure incurred on each of the following items, separately for each item:

(a) Consumption of stores and spare parts.
(b) Power and fuel.
(c) Rent.
(d) Repairs to buildings.
(e) Repairs to machinery.
(f) (i) Salaries, wages and bonus.
(ii) Contribution to provident and other funds.
(iii) Workmen and staff welfare expenses (to the extent not adjusted from any previous provision or reserve).

15. (a) The amount of income from investments, distinguishing between trade investments and other investments.
(b) Other income by way of interest, specifying the nature of the income.
(c) The amount of income tax deducted if the gross income is stated under sub-paragraphs (a) and (b) above.

16. (a) Profits or losses on investments showing distinctly the extent of the profit, or losses earned or incurred on account of membership of a partnership firm, to the extent not adjusted from any previous provision or reserve.
(b) Profits or losses in respect of transactions of a kind, not usually undertaken by the company or undertaken in circumstances of an exceptional or non-recurring nature, if material in amount.
(c) Miscellaneous income.

17. (a) Dividends from subsidiary companies.
(b) Provisions for losses of subsidiary companies.

18. The aggregate amount of the dividends paid and proposed, and stating whether such amounts are subject to deduction of income tax or not.

19. Effect of any changes in the basis of accounting, if material.

In addition to the above information, further disclosure is required. The profit and loss account shall also contain or give by way of a note detailed information showing separately the following payments provided or made during the financial year to the directors (including managing director), or managers, if any, by (a) the company, (b) the subsidiaries of the company and (c) any other person:

1. Managerial remuneration, under s. 198 of the Act paid or payable during the financial year to the directors (including managing director) or managers, if any.
2. Other allowances and commissions, including guarantee commission (details to be given).
3. Any other perquisites or benefits in cash or in kind (stating approximate money value where practicable).
4. Pensions, etc.
   (a) Pension.
   (b) Gratuities.
   (c) Payment from provident fund, in excess of own subscriptions and interest thereon.
   (d) Consideration in connection with retirement from office.

The profit and loss account must give or contain by way of a note a statement showing the computation of net profits in accordance with s. 349 of the Companies Act with relevant details of the calculation of the commissions payable by way of percentages of such profits to the directors (including managing director) or managers, if any. This section lays down rules for computing net profit in cases where directors' remuneration is dependent thereon.

The profit and loss account must also contain or give by way of a note detailed information as regards amounts paid to the auditor, whether as fees or otherwise for services rendered:

1. As auditor.
2. As advisor, or in any other capacity, in respect of,
   (i) Taxation matters.
   (ii) Company law matters.
   (iii) Management services.
3. In any other manner.

In addition to the above disclosure certain production information and details of foreign currency transactions must be given. The detailed requirements are described elsewhere in this study.

The above details of specific information to be disclosed are supplemented by the requirement to disclose certain items constituting miscellaneous expenditure. It was found that the item 'miscellaneous expenditure' in the profit and loss account concealed fairly heavy amounts of expenditure for which separate disclosure was not required under the provisions of Part II of Schedule VI to the Companies Act. An amendment to the Act provides that any item of expenditure which exceeds 1 per cent of the total revenue or 5,000 rupees, whichever is higher, should be disclosed separately in the profit and loss account under an appropriate caption. This disclosure requirement has differing results in different companies as a variety of items may fall into the disclosure category. An example of disclosure of miscellaneous expenditure can be seen in Figure 3.7 of the accounts of National Organic Chemical Industries Limited.

These disclosure requirements are, in certain respects, in excess of those of the United Kingdom. This results from the need of the Indian government to control and monitor the growth of industry.

SUMMARY

This Chapter has discussed the topic of information disclosure in Indian financial reports. The relevant statutory requirements have been considered along with the pronouncements of the Institute of Chartered Accountants of India. The situation in India has been compared with that in the United Kingdom. Information obtained from the author's survey, the survey of the Institute of Chartered Accountants of India (1981) and earlier work by Das Gupta (1977) and Singhvi (1967) has been incorporated into the discussion.

Overall, the disclosure of information in financial reports in India does not appear to be as comprehensive as in the United Kingdom. However there are many similarities and the accounting standards programme of the Indian Institute will cause the gap to narrow as more companies adopt the recommendations. The Indian disclosure of production capacity and consumption of raw materials is one area that is notably in excess of United Kingdom requirements. The probable explanation of this is the different economic and political environment. India is a developing country that is making some attempts at planning its economy by modifying the basic framework of capitalism and free enterprise.

Figure 3.7
NATIONAL ORGANIC CHEMICAL INDUSTRIES LIMITED

Schedules forming part of Profit and Loss Account for the year ended 31st December, 1982

SCHEDULE 16: MANUFACTURING AND OTHER EXPENSES

	1982 Rupees in lakhs	1981 Rupees in lakhs
Raw Materials Consumed	64,76.53	73,01.51
Process Chemicals Consumed	11,99.66	8,63.84
Purchases of Trading Products	7,32.60	6,25.82
Stores Consumed	96.01	78.07
Obsolete Stores written off	2.02	49.95
Storage, Packing and Octroi	2,41.36	2,29.39
Power and Fuel	17,38.45	16,09.07
Other Utilities	68.57	60.84
Salaries, Wages and Bonus	6,69.09	5,98.89
Contribution to Provident and other Funds	82.34	81.69
Staff Welfare	1,07.59	89.89
Rent	51.04	59.27
Repairs and Maintenance to Plant and Machinery	6,25.90	4,70.10
Repairs and Maintenance to Buildings	39.05	25.27
Insurance	1,27.59	89.23
Rates and Taxes	50.95	36.82
Commission and Discounts	1,22.46	1,28.83
Royalties and Service Charges	50.00	50.00
Directors' Fees	0.34	0.25
Directors' Commission	-	3.73
Value of Minor Fixed Assets written off	3.13	0.96
Loss on disposal of Fixed Assets (Net)	0.10	8.23
Loss on Sale of Investments	-	0.01
Obsolete Plant and Machinery written off	6.81	8.99
Debenture Issue Expenses written off	0.21	-
Premium on Debenture Redemption	0.72	-
Miscellaneous Expenses	5,71.02	4,31.35
	130,63.54	129,02.00
Less: Amount Capitalised	50.39	29.83
TOTAL	130,13.15	128,72.17

Miscellaneous Expenses include expenses relating to staff recruitment and training, postage, telephone, telegrams, printing and stationery, travelling, motor cars, entertainment, professional charges, donations and contributions, staff housing, etc.

Figure 3.7 (cont'd)

SCHEDULE 17: INTEREST

	1982 Rupees in lakhs	1981 Rupees in lakhs
On Debentures	17.75	-
On Fixed Loans and Deposits	3,44.59	3,37.91
Others	5,92.39	3,07.56
TOTAL	9,54.73	6,45.47

(1) Reproduced by permission of The Institute of Chartered Accountants of India.

Chapter Four

SOCIAL AND NON-FINANCIAL INFORMATION DISCLOSURE

INTRODUCTION

In both the United Kingdom and India company law has seemed to stress the importance of reporting to shareholders on the stewardship of management. In recent years however there has been discussion of the wider responsibility of enterprises to account for their activities to different groups of stakeholders such as employees, the government and society at large. The publication of 'The Corporate Report' by the Accounting Standards Committee (1975) generated interest in the United Kingdom and the publication of a Value-Added Statement has become fairly widespread as a result. In India various developments in company law have increased disclosure requirements in certain areas of special interest to government in its desire to control and monitor the growth of large-scale industry. The requirement to report detailed information about highly paid employees and production capacity information disclosure can be cited as examples. Since independence India has been attempting to develop and strengthen its industrial base. This has led to import controls and a protected home market. The Foreign Exchange Regulation Act, 1973 (FERA) restricts inward investment and foreign equity participation in certain industries. The company law requirements to disclose imports, exports, expenditure in foreign currency and the amount remitted during the year in foreign currencies on account of dividends arise from government's concern to control these areas.

In addition to the legal requirements to disclose information that can broadly be described to be of a social nature a certain amount of voluntary disclosure has arisen in India. A similar trend has been observed in the United Kingdom. The directors' report and chairman's statement increasingly contain qualitative remarks and quantitative information of a social nature. This chapter will show the extent to which social accounting developments have occurred.

VALUE-ADDED REPORTING AND DISTRIBUTION OF REVENUE STATEMENTS

Publication of Value-Added Statements has become fairly widespread in the United Kingdom since the Corporate Report of 1975. Some companies in India have published these statements. The survey of the Institute of Chartered Accountants of India gives two examples of statements published but does not comment on this development. Das Gupta (1977, p. 177) comments that in the annual reports of many companies information has been given in the form of a bar diagram, picture or graph as to 'how the rupee was earned and spent' and 'distribution of earnings'.

The author's survey found that only two companies gave a statement of value-added, however a more popular statement was of distribution of revenue generally shown in diagrammatic form. Twelve companies gave this information. An example of this type of statement can be seen in Table 4.1.

Table 4.1
The Tata Oil Mills Company Limited

DISTRIBUTION OF REVENUE

	1982/83		1981/82	
	Rs/crores	%	Rs/crores	%
Raw materials	101.17	59.8	103.96	64.1
Operation & other expenses	21.09	12.5	18.48	11.4
Income tax & excise duty	16.12	9.6	12.90	8.0
Employees	14.76	8.7	12.79	7.9
Freight, advertising & selling expenses	11.21	6.6	10.39	6.4
Profits	3.24	1.9	2.14	1.3
Depreciation	1.55	0.9	1.40	0.9
	169.14	100.0	162.06	100.0

EMPLOYMENT INFORMATION REPORTING

The requirement for disclosure of non-monetary information in the financial statements of companies was introduced in 1971 and the scope of the requirements were widened in 1973. The Companies Act, 1956 was amended to include the new rules which contain provisions relating to employment information. At present information regarding higher paid employees is to be submitted by all categories of companies. The profit and loss account should contain by way of a note details of expenditure on salaries, wages, bonus and contribution to provident and other funds on employees in receipt of remuneration aggregating to at least 36,000 rupees per annum. In the case of those employed for part of the year disclosure is required if remuneration is at least 3,000 rupees per month. Disclosure is also required with regard to the number of employees falling into each of the above categories. Remuneration includes the value of any perquisites, the monetary value of these are to be calculated in accordance with income tax law. An example from the accounts of the Indian Tube Company Limited can be seen in Figure 4.2.

Figure 4.2
Schedule forming part of the profit and loss account.

Break-up of the expenditure incurred during the year on employees who were in receipt of remuneration for the year not less than Rs 36,000 in the aggregate or at the rate of Rs 3,000 per month -

	Employed throughout the financial year		Employed for a part of the financial year	
	1982/83 Rupees Lakhs	1981/82 Rupees Lakhs	1982/83 Rupees Lakhs	1981/82 Rupees Lakhs
(1) Expenditure	75.54	59.99	2.37	3.66
Salaries and bonus retirement benefits	16.84	12.93	0.45	1.09
Value of perquisites	11.84	8.64	0.28	0.53
	104.22	81.56	3.10	5.28
(2) Number of employees	221	176	13	18

The disclosure requirement shown in Table 4.2 is more extensive than the corresponding United Kingdom requirement to state the number of higher paid employees in bands. In addition the Indian Companies Act requires an annexure to the directors' report. This is a detailed statement giving the name, age, designation/nature of duties, remuneration received/receivable, qualifications, date of commencement of employment and last employment held before joining the company (name of employer and designation) of all highly paid employees. Some companies state that the employees have adequate experience to discharge their duties. The relationship of employees with the directors must be indicated. This statement can be many pages long in the case of a large company and is a disclosure requirement far in excess of those generally encountered in other countries.

Disclosure of directors' remuneration is less extensive than in the United Kingdom. Only the total directors' remuneration needs to be shown compared with the United Kingdom disclosure of chairman's and highest paid director's remuneration and the number of directors receiving remuneration in bands of five thousand pounds.

Indian directors' reports do sometimes provide additional descriptive and quantitative information regarding employees. An example from the directors' report of the State of Trading Corporation of India Limited can be seen in Figure 4.3.

Figure 4.3

Personnel and Welfare

As required under the provisions of section 217(2A) of Companies Act, 1956, a statement showing particulars of employees drawing remuneration of more than Rs 3,000 per month is annexed to the Report. None of the employees mentioned therein is related to any Director of the Corporation.

Industrial relations remain fairly cordial during the year. Proposals for revision of pay scales and allowances in respect of Managers are under the consideration of Government.

About 150 Managers and staff were deputed to various outside training programmes, seminars and conferences, including three Managers to training programmes abroad. Besides, nine in-company training programmes were

> arranged in collaboration with reputed institutions in the areas of International Trade, Market Research, Export Finance, Shipping and Insurance. Nine Management Trainees from different disciplines were recruited.
>
> The Corporation continued its efforts to encourage progressive use of Hindi in its offices situated in non-Hindi speaking areas, through adequate arrangements for teaching Hindi. Besides organising workshops on Hindi, official language week was also observed. The scheme of training in Hindi stenography and typing continued to attract more and more employees of the Corporation.
>
> In our endeavour to fill up the back-log in managerial and staff cadres, exclusive advertisements were issued and vacancies earmarked for SC/ST, including very senior positions were filled. The developmental training programmes for SC/ST employees have been further expanded.
>
> The Corporation continued to recruit staff from ex-servicemen against reservations made for them. Details of recruitment under this scheme are given elsewhere in the Annual Report.
>
> (SC = scheduled castes   ST = scheduled tribes)

Some companies provide information in the form of charts and diagrams. The Indian Tube Company Limited shows the growth in average earnings per employee over a ten year period. This information could have been more useful if information regarding inflation had also been provided.

SOCIAL INFORMATION REPORTING

The survey of the Institute of Chartered Accountants of India found evidence that company management is becoming increasingly aware of social and community causes. One hundred and twenty-three out of 202 companies provided information, through the directors' report, on the company contribution in this regard. The findings are summarised in Table 4.4

One company made an attempt to account for human resources. This consisted of a statement of human asset values and a professional profile of the workforce. One company gave a statement of monetary exchanges with government. Quite a few companies gave details of shareholdings showing the number of shareholders and their sub-division by the number of shares held.

Table 4.4
Social Responsibility Accounting (1)

Item	Number of Companies
Employee welfare	47
Donation for social causes	28
Spreading education	14
Aid in national distress	12
Family planning and health	12
Employment growth	3
Workers' participation in management	2
Pollution control	1

The author's survey of thirty companies found a large number of references to industrial relations. The results are shown in Table 4.5.

Table 4.5
Social Responsibility Accounting

Item	Number of Companies
Industrial relations	28
Community involvement	12
Education and research	10
Breakdown of shareholders	5
Encouragement of use of Hindi	4
Energy saving	3
Pollution control	3
Expenditure on social overheads	2
Money exchanges with government	2
Employment of disadvantaged groups	2
Charitable donations	2
Human resources	1
Safety	1

Indian Airlines Limited and Bharat Earth Movers Limited gave statements of expenditure on social overheads and an example is shown in Figure 4.6. A typical comment on industrial relations is given below from the accounts of the Indian Cable Company Limited:

Cordial industrial relations prevailed

throughout the year at all locations. In my statement last year I had made mention of the signing of the new agreement with the recognised workers' union at Jamshedpur and that negotiations were under way with other unions. I am glad to inform you that the new memorandum of settlement with the Federation for Pune Works, Branches and Calcutta office was also signed. With the conclusion of these agreements we look forward to substantial improvement in productivity at all units which is so vital for the Company to face the recession period now being witnessed in the Cable Industry.

Figure 4.6
Extract from the Annual Report of Indian Airlines Limited

Statement of Expenditure on Social Overheads

Particulars	31-3-1982 Rupees	31-3-1981 Rupees
1. Expenditure on Township including Depreciation on Housing Colony	42,30,321	42,02,475
2. Maintenance of Schools and Educational Facilities	6,90,598	6,22,605
3. Provision of Medical facilities over and above those which are statutorily required to be maintained by the undertaking	1,37,17,021	1,07,26,723
4. Provision of Subsidised Transport	11,92,871	11,37,400
5. Subsidy in regard to Social and Cultural Activities	4,71,353	3,93,543
	2,03,02,164	1,70,82,746
Less: Recoveries from staff on account of Township	10,22,231	12,38,050
Net	1,92,79,933	1,58,44,696

The following note (Figure 4.7) from the Chairman's report of Larsen and Toubro is of interest as it deals with health issues and family planning, a topic of great social concern in India.

Figure 4.7

The foundation of any business enterprise is the character of its people. A business succeeds and grows in the long-term on the basis of respect and concern for its employees, the community in which it operates and the public it serves.

We, in L & T, have a firm belief in the values of human development and our social obligation to not only our employees, but also to the community.

The medical and social welfare activities conducted through our Andheri Welfare Centre are much appreciated. These services covering general medicine, gynaecology, obstetrics, family planning, paediatrics, dermatological and dental care, etc. are extended to the neighbouring community. Special emphasis is placed on family planning campaigns organised on a regular basis in the last three years. With the increasing interest created amongst the families of the employees and the community, the response has been extremely good. One thousand three hundred and twenty-eight sterilisation operations have been performed in the past year.

L & T is the recipient of the Shri S.M. Dahanukar Trophy for welfare activities in engineering industries for 1981.

We are pursuing our efforts to improve productivity in L & Ts operations. Attitudes of introspection are encouraged. Our 'suggestion scheme' is a source of great value in our operations.

An example of a note regarding progressive use of Hindi is given in Figure 4.8 from the accounts of the Indian Farmers Fertiliser Co-operative Limited. The adoption of Hindi as opposed to English is an element of government policy that is being resisted in non-Hindi speaking areas of the country and legislation is being introduced to enforce the use of Hindi in various cases.

Figure 4.8

Progressive Use of Hindi

In pursuance of the provisions of the Official Language

Figure 4.8 (cont'd)

Act and Rules, efforts were continued to develop the progressive use of Hindi in IFFCO and the following steps were taken during the year.

In compliance of the minimum programme drawn out for the year, all the Name Places, Sign Boards, Rubber Stamps, Letter Heads, Forms and Headings of Registers, Stationery items, etc. were prepared in bi-lingual form. All letters received in Hindi were replied in Hindi. All orders under the Industrial Employment (Standing Orders) Act, 1946 and other Labour Laws, all Notices and Circulars of standing nature are also being issued bi-lingually. Byelaws, Annual Report, Chairman's Speech, Budget Estimates, Agenda and Proceedings of Annual General Meeting as also official papers to be laid before Parliament are also being issued both in Hindi and English. 'IFFCO SAMACHAR' a quarterly magazine is being printed in Hindi and English and a Hindi chapter has been added to the 'IFFCO NEWS', a house magazine issued bi-monthly. Society's 'Logo' has been prepared in Hindi in addition to English. Steps have also been taken to print the fertiliser bags in both the languages.

Apart from the Head Office, Hindi units have been set up in all the three Plants and Zonal Offices of the Society. For encouraging English typists and stenographers to do Hindi typing and stenography work along with their normal duties, an incentive scheme has been introduced. Officers and employees who do not have working knowledge of Hindi are being sponsored to undergo training in Hindi, in a phased manner. For those having working knowledge of Hindi, workshops were held to train them for using Hindi in their noting and drafting. For monitoring the development of Hindi, Official Language Implementation Committees have been constituted in the Head Office, Plants, Zonal and State Offices. During the year under report, the Committee of Parliament on Official Language visited our offices at Bombay, Bangalore and Madras.

The disclosure of share distribution is illustrated by an extract (Figure 4.9) from the accounts of Union Carbide India Limited.

In conclusion it can be seen that social information reporting in India is developing voluntarily amongst some of the large progressive companies.

Figure 4.9
Extract from the Accounts of Union Carbide India Limited

Share Distribution

Block of Shares	1982 Number of Shareholders	%	1981 Number of Shareholders	%
1 to 10	1410	5.92	921	3.92
11 to 20	525	2.21	493	2.10
21 to 50	2549	10.71	2404	10.25
51 to 100	3958	16.63	3779	16.11
101 to 500	11657	48.98	12004	51.17
501 to 1000	2109	8.86	2188	9.32
1001 and above	1592	6.69	1672	7.13
	23800	100.00	23461	100.00

SUMMARY

This Chapter has been concerned with the disclosure of social and other non-financial information in Indian financial reporting. The situation in India has been compared with that in the United Kingdom. The relevant legislation has been described. However, there are no accounting standards relating to this topic. The results of the author's survey and the survey of the Institute of Chartered Accountants of India have been incorporated into the discussion.

It appears that there is a growing awareness of the need to report on social matters in both countries. In the United Kingdom the value-added statement is a popular form of voluntary disclosure. The adoption of such statements in India may be the result of the United Kingdom influence. The extensive disclosures relating to higher paid employees in India are in contrast to the minimal information required in the United Kingdom. The different political environment provides a probable explanation of this. India is a developing country with a great need to develop and use its human resources in order to raise the standard of living. The required disclosures thus meet the needs of government and society at large. At the same time, in both countries disclosure of social information is being made voluntarily. Companies are presumably aware of the growing demands of society and are making an attempt to provide relevant information.

Social accounting is an area that is still in its infancy. Further developments can be expected as governments introduce legislation and professional bodies develop guidelines. Since the United Kingdom is a developed country and India is a less developed country there will probably be different developments in social accounting in these countries in the future to reflect different social concerns.

(1) Reproduced by permission of The Institute of Chartered Accountants of India.

Chapter Five

INDIAN FINANCIAL REPORTING : AN EMPIRICAL ANALYSIS

INTRODUCTION

The quality of financial reporting in a country depends on the legal requirements governing disclosure together with professional recommendations which may have a varying degree of effectiveness depending on the influence of the professional bodies. Stock exchange requirements may add to the content of the financial reports of quoted companies.

Traditionally the aim of financial statements has been to provide information for investors. Investors need to assess the financial position, profitability and future prospects of a company. Other user groups also have an interest in financial reports and their information requirements may differ from those of the investor group.

In examining the quality of financial reporting in India the legal requirements have been considered along with the accounting standards and guidance notes of the Institute of Chartered Accountants of India. To supplement this descriptive information, it was decided to carry out a survey of a number of recent annual reports of Indian companies. In addition, the results of previous surveys by Singhvi (1967), Das Gupta (1977) and the research committee of the Institute of Chartered Accountants of India (1981) have been reviewed and discussed in the preceding sections. The methodology and results of the author's survey will be discussed below.

METHODOLOGY

In assessing the quality of Indian financial disclosure it was decided to use an index of disclosure suggested by M. Edgar Barret (1976). This index is reproduced in Appendix D and contains seventeen categories of information. The items were chosen by Barrett partly on the basis of earlier studies of disclosure in American annual reports by Cerf (1965), Singhvi and Desai (1971) and Buzby (1974) and partly on the basis of personal experience in dealing with foreign financial statements and their users. There is a degree of arbitrariness inherent in the use of a weighted index, both in the selection of items and the size of the weightings. However, the technique does provide a useful starting point in the assessment of the quality of the disclosure.

The names of the Indian companies surveyed were obtained from Dun and Bradstreet International. It was decided to concentrate on large companies as these were considered most likely to represent the best current accounting practice in India. Accordingly sixty-three companies were selected, being all those with a turnover of over five hundred million rupees. Letters were written to these companies requesting a copy of the most recent annual report. Thirty of these companies responded and these formed the basis of the survey. The reports obtained had year ends in 1982 and 1983 and covered a wide variety of industries. The names and periods of the annual reports are listed in Appendix E.

An index score was calculated for each company surveyed and the score was converted to a percentage of the maximum possible score taking into account the fact some of the disclosure items were not applicable to certain companies.

In the following cases some departure from the maximum points for the items of information were possible. Decisions on these items are as stated:

Item 3. Segment reporting : Geographical area - Sales. One mark was awarded if a figure for exports was given with no further qualification.

Item 5. Capital expenditure : Planned. One mark was awarded if a figure for the estimated amount of contracts remaining to be executed on capital account and not provided for was given in the notes to the accounts with no further information.

Item 6. Depreciation method. Two marks were awarded if the accounts stated that depreciation was provided in accordance with the provisions of the Companies Act without actually specifying the method.

Item 14. Depreciation life. Two marks were awarded if the accounts stated that depreciation was provided in accordance with the provisions of the Companies Act without actually specifying the asset life or rates used. One mark was awarded where the life of only one type of asset was specifically stated and reference was made to 'estimated useful lives' of other assets. In another case one mark was awarded where it was stated 'Depreciation is provided ... at rates not less than those required under section 205(2)(b) of the Companies Act, 1956'.

The results of the survey are given in the following section along with a comparison with the United Kingdom. It was not considered necessary to carry out an independent survey of British companies as the annual surveys carried out by the Institute of Chartered Accountants of England and Wales for 1982/83 and 1983/84 were used to provide the necessary information on levels of disclosure.

In assessing the comparability of the United Kingdom and Indian companies selected in the samples it was noted that the United Kingdom companies were generally larger. The United Kingdom 1982/83 survey sample included companies in the top 500 of The Times 1000 with turnovers ranging from twenty-five thousand million pounds to eighty million pounds. The 1983/84 survey included companies in the top 750 of The Times 1000 with turnovers over fifty-two million pounds. The Indian companies selected had turnovers ranging from one thousand three hundred million pounds to twelve million pounds approximately. Although the comparison was carried out between samples of companies of different sizes in terms of turnover this was not considered to invalidate the comparison since the Indian companies selected for the sample were amongst the largest and most important in that country.

RESULTS

After converting the index scores to percentages for the thirty Indian companies surveyed, a mean score of 62.45 was calculated (Appendix F). This score can be compared with the disclosure of United Kingdom companies which was measured by Barrett (1976) in 1968 and 1972. The results are displayed in Table 5.1.

Table 5.1
Disclosure in United Kingdom Annual Reports

	UK 1968	UK 1972	India 1982/83
Index score	63.6%	73.1%	62.4%
Number of companies in sample	15	15	30

It appears therefore that the level of disclosure in current Indian financial reports is roughly similar to that of United Kingdom accounts in the late 1960s.

However, the level of disclosure in the United Kingdom is now substantially higher than at the time of Barrett's work, largely because of the development of the profession's accounting standards programme and because certain companies make voluntary disclosures in advance of standards. This conjecture will be substantiated by considering the results of the survey of United Kingdom published accounts carried out by the Institute of Chartered Accountants in England and Wales (1983 and 1984). The various items of information in Barrett's disclosure index were considered. In some cases the information in the survey could not be compared directly with the index items. Appendix G sets out the levels of disclosure from the 1982/83 survey. These results relate to accounts issued during the year to 30 June 1982. The Indian accounts surveyed have year ends ranging from 31 March 1982 to 31 July 1983. It was therefore considered appropriate to review the United Kingdom levels of disclosure for the subsequent survey 1983/84 which included accounts issued in the year to 30 June 1983. The results from the 1983/84 survey are set out in Appendix H. Certain items of information were not covered by this survey due to a change in editorial policy. It was decided that some aspects of financial reporting practices would be surveyed less frequently than others.

The United Kingdom company reports in the 1982/83 and 1983/84 surveys were not subject to the requirements of the 1981 Companies Act which applies to accounting years beginning on or after 15 June 1982. The majority of the items in the disclosure index were already covered by existing British legal requirements or accounting standards. However, the additional disclosure of gross margin will be required under the 1981 Companies Act if the operational profit and loss format is adopted. This survey then compares Indian accounts with pre-1981 Companies Act United Kingdom accounts and this fact must be borne in mind when interpreting the results.

It was not possible to calculate a mean index of disclosure score for United Kingdom companies from the information given in the surveys. However, it was possible to compare the numbers of companies disclosing most of the items of information. Appendix I sets out the percentages of Indian and United Kingdom companies disclosing the various items of information. Tests were carried out to discover whether the differences in observed percentages of companies disclosing certain items of information were statistically significant. The notes to Appendix I give the results of these tests. On examination of the results set out in Appendix I it was noted that in respect of five of the items of information the level of disclosure was the same in both countries. This was due to the existence of similar legal requirements. The United Kingdom companies disclosed significantly more in respect of seven items. On the other hand, the level of disclosure was higher in India in respect of five items. In the case of four of these items this was due to an Indian legal requirement in excess of that in the United Kingdom.

The following explanations relate to the seven items for which United Kingdom companies give greater disclosure:

<u>Item 2</u>. Segment reporting : Product line - Operating results. This is explained by the stock exchange listing agreement requirements on segmental reporting.

<u>Items 6 and 14</u>. Depreciation method and life. This is explained by the existence of an accounting standard (SSAP12).

<u>Item 7</u>. Funds flow statement. This is explained by the existence of an accounting standard (SSAP10).

<u>Item 11</u>. Price level adjusted statements. This is explained by the existence of an accounting standard (SSAP16).

<u>Items 13 and 15</u>. Currency translation method and foreign exchange gains and losses. This is

explained by the existence of an accounting standard exposure draft (ED27).

To support the contention that the level of disclosure in the United Kingdom has increased since Barrett (1976) calculated disclosure scores, it was decided to compute the index score for a company complying with legal requirements, stock exchange requirements, accounting standards and exposure drafts in existence at the time of the Institute's 1982/83 survey. A company complying with, but not exceeding, the above items would obtain an index score of 49 or 86.7%.

To summarise the above observations, it appears that Indian financial disclosure exceeds that in the United Kingdom when the Indian company law requirements are more demanding than those in the United Kingdom. Initially Indian company law was very similar to that of Britain. However, developments since independence have resulted in differences as the Indian legislators have introduced regulations to meet the needs of the environment. United Kingdom disclosure exceeds that in India when the profession's accounting standards introduce requirements in excess of the legal minimum. India also has an accounting standards programme which is very similar to that of the United Kingdom but the Indian standards are as yet only recommendations. These observations relate to the disclosure of seventeen selected items of information. There are many other types of information disclosure that could be compared and thus only tentative conclusions can be drawn from the results.

In addition to making a comparison with the United Kingdom, it was decided to determine the extent to which Indian companies exceed the minimum legal disclosure requirements. Appendix J considers the various items of information in the disclosure index and the notes indicate what the legal disclosure requirement is. A company merely complying with the legal requirements would receive an index score of 26 or 46.0%. This is somewhat lower than the mean score achieved of 35.1 or 62.4%. The actual scores achieved ranged from 49.6% to 83.2% indicating that no companies were disclosing less than the legal minimum whilst some companies were disclosing far more than the minimum. One reason for disclosing more than the minimum could be the overriding requirement for the accounts to give a true and fair view. Also the accounting standards programme of the Institute of Chartered Accountants of India could be a contributing factor in conjunction with a desire by management to provide more information for investors and other users. It is interesting to note that both of the highest scoring companies were government owned and that the company in third place was a co-operative venture.

The results of the author's survey are therefore in accordance with the conclusions of the research committee of the Institute of Chartered Accountants of India (1981) who noted:

> A significant feature of the published accounts was that much greater information than strictly required by law was being given.

This result can be contrasted with Singhvi's (1967) earlier conclusion that:

> Most of the annual reports examined here do not disclose more information than what is required by law.

SUMMARY

This Chapter has described the author's survey of financial disclosure by Indian companies. A sample of thirty of India's largest companies was taken and an index of disclosure score determined for each company. The index of disclosure used was that developed by Barrett (1976). The mean disclosure score for the sample of Indian companies was shown to be equivalent to that achieved by United Kingdom companies in the late 1960s. The individual items in the index were then considered and a comparison was made between the proportion of Indian and United Kingdom companies disclosing. Statistical tests were employed to determine whether differences in levels of disclosure were significant. The information on United Kingdom disclosure was obtained from the survey of the Institute of Chartered Accountants in England and Wales (1983) and (1984). A notional index score was calculated for a United Kingdom company complying with all relevant requirements in existence at the time of the survey. This was much higher than that observed by Barrett (1976) for United Kingdom companies in the late 1960s and by the author for Indian companies at present.

The comparison of individual index items disclosed that for some items levels of disclosure were the same in both countries. For the remaining items the level of disclosure was higher either in the United Kingdom or India. The reasons for differences in disclosure of the various items were then considered. It was concluded that where Indian disclosure exceeded that in the United Kingdom it was mainly due to legal requirements. Where United Kingdom disclosure exceeded that in India it was mainly due to the requirements of the accounting standards.

The results of the survey were also used to establish the extent to which Indian companies exceed the minimum legal disclosure requirements. It was found that companies were giving more information than that strictly required by the law. In some cases a great deal of extra information was being given.

In conclusion it can be said that disclosure in the United Kingdom was greater than in India at the time of the survey. This is in respect of the particular index of disclosure selected. The construction of an index of disclosure involves a certain amount of subjectivity hence any conclusions drawn about the overall level of disclosure in both countries can only be tentative. If the accounting standards programme of the Institute of Chartered Accountants of India gains acceptance the level of disclosure and similarity with the United Kingdom will doubtless increase.

Chapter Six

SUMMARY AND CONCLUSIONS

This study has been concerned with the field of international accounting. It was decided to select a less developed country, India, and to describe the financial reporting practices in the commercial sector. As India was for many years a part of the British Empire, it was expected that there would be a significant influence on its financial reporting practices. A comparison of Indian and United Kingdom accounting was carried out to ascertain the similarities and differences between the two countries.

Financial reporting practices in a country are determined by a variety of environmental factors. Prior to a detailed discussion of financial reporting in India and the United Kingdom, it was decided to examine the various factors that might affect accounting practices. The economic, political and cultural environment of India was compared with that of the United Kingdom. Since India is a less developed country and the United Kingdom is a developed western country, many differences in the environment were observed. The historical links between the two countries did however lead to certain similarities. India has adopted the system of parliamentary democracy in contrast with many other third world countries where one party systems, dictatorships and military rule are common. India also has a large industrial sector in world terms with a diversity of industries. Unlike the United Kingdom however there has been a greater degree of government control and protectionism. India's use of five-year plans is reminiscent of the methods adopted by Soviet bloc countries.

Environmental factors that might be expected to have a direct impact on financial reporting practices were then considered in detail. The legal environments of the two countries were found to display similarities. Company law forms the basis for Indian financial reporting as it does in the United Kingdom. Company law prior to independence was very similar. Since then Indian law has been subject to revisions relating to financial reporting. The result of this is that there are disclosure requirements in India in excess of those in the United Kingdom. Some of these additions to financial reporting requirements would seem to meet the need of the Indian government to assess and regulate the performance of industry. In the United Kingdom the directives of the European Community have affected company law and will continue to do so. The legal environment in the two countries is thus likely to become more dissimilar in future. In many countries the tax laws have a great influence on financial reporting practices. For example, the published profit figure may have to be calculated according to tax regulations. In both the United Kingdom and India this is not the case, taxable profits are calculated by adjusting reported profit figures. Thus tax legislation does not have a great effect on financial reporting practices.

The existence of stock exchanges where members of the public can trade in securities may have an effect on financial reporting practices. The stock exchange may impose its own regulations on companies with a quotation in order to protect investors and satisfy their perceived information needs. There is a great need for capital in developing countries and the existence of well regulated, efficient stock exchanges can help to satisfy this need. The development of the Indian stock exchanges from early times to the present day exhibits similarities with the situation in the United Kingdom. Nowadays the main Indian stock exchanges are reputable institutions subject to strict government legislation. There is evidence to indicate that semi-strong efficiency exists as it does in the United Kingdom. In the United Kingdom the stock exchange listing agreement has from time to time imposed additional information disclosure requirements on companies. This can be contrasted with the situation in India where the legal requirements are considered to be sufficient and have not been extended by the stock exchanges.

The ability of professional associations of accountants to influence financial reporting practices depends on the status and power of a profession within a particular country. In some countries government regulation of financial reporting leaves little scope for the profession to influence matters. In both the United Kingdom and India however the accountancy profession has a significant influence on financial reporting practices. The Institute of Chartered Accountants of India is modelled closely on that in the United Kingdom. The accounting standards programme in India is clearly following the lead of the United Kingdom. There is more government control in India as the Chartered Accountants Act of 1949 lays down rules for the conduct of the Institute and the discipline of members.

Academics working in institutes of higher education can affect the financial reporting practices in a country. They can carry out research and enter into a dialogue with practitioners. Individuals can divide their time between academic posts and professional work. The educational establishments produce graduates and diploma holders with an initial training in accountancy who will then proceed to membership of professional bodies or to work as accounting technicians. In both India and the United Kingdom the academic community can be considered an important factor. Research is carried out in both countries in many establishments. Conditions in Indian universities and colleges are, however, far from ideal and this factor may hamper research to a certain extent.

After considering the various factors in the accounting environments of the two countries, it was concluded that there were many basic similarities. This tends to support the initial assumption that financial reporting practices in India will be influenced by those in the United Kingdom. The following Chapters then considered the financial reporting practices in India in detail and made comparisons with the United Kingdom.

In examining the detailed financial reporting practices in India use was made of a variety of publications. The Indian Companies Act of 1956 and the various publications of the Institute of Chartered Accountants were referred to. The author carried out a survey of the accounts of thirty large Indian companies. In addition the results of previous surveys by Singhvi (1967), Das Gupta (1977) and the research committee of the Institute of Chartered Accountants of India (1981) were referred to.

The topic of income measurement and asset valuation was considered. It was noted that in both the United Kingdom and India, company law leaves a large amount of freedom to companies in determination of accounting policies. Accounting standards in both countries have attempted to increase uniformity in certain areas. Two major areas of importance in asset valuation that were considered were fixed assets and inventory. There were similarities in the treatment of these items. However, the level of disclosure was higher in the United Kingdom and companies showed more uniformity in their practices. It was notable that inflation accounting in India has not progressed very far although the Institute has adopted the approach of the United Kingdom accounting standard (SSAP16) into its own programme as a guidance note. Another important area was preparation of group accounts. Whereas United Kingdom groups of companies almost invariably prepare consolidated accounts such a procedure is a rarity in India. Companies present the accounts of subsidiaries along with the accounts of the holding company. This presentation is feasible because Indian companies do not form themselves into very large groups.

The developments in the debate on foreign currency translation that have occurred in the United Kingdom and the United States do not appear to have influenced the situation in India. Since Indian companies do not provide world-wide consolidations the situation is rather different from that in the United Kingdom. The Indian Institute issued a statement in 1976 advocating a hybrid of the current/non-current method and no accounting standard has yet been issued. This statement advocated disclosure of the accounting policy and translation differences dealt with through the profit and loss account and otherwise. Indian companies however do not yet show a high degree of disclosure in this area.

The amount and quality of information disclosed in annual reports varies from country to country. Disclosure may be voluntary or enforced by law or professional regulations. It might be expected that disclosure in the United Kingdom would be greater overall than in India. It seems logical to expect that a developed country with a complex economy and sophisticated markets for capital would display a higher level of disclosure than a less developed country. The need for improved disclosure has been recognised in the accounting standards programme of the Institute of Chartered Accountants of India. The influence of the United Kingdom is apparent in the accounting standards on disclosure of accounting policies and accounting for changes in financial position. However as accounting standards in India are only recommendations compliance is by no means universal.

Indian companies regularly provide financial histories and simplified accounts as part of the annual report. This is an area of voluntary disclosure that is similar to that in the United Kingdom, although Indian companies favour giving longer financial histories. It was found that segmental reporting was not highly developed in India. The legal requirements were more modest than those in the United Kingdom and the amount of voluntary disclosure was fairly small. In the case of forecast information neither country requires formal profits forecasts as part of the annual report but qualitative comments about future prospects are fairly common in the directors' and chairman's reports. The system of licensing production in India leads to additional disclosure requirements. The licensed production capacity, the actual production and a detailed break-down of raw materials consumed must be disclosed in Indian accounts. Also the value of imports of raw materials, components and capital goods must be disclosed. These disclosures are not required in the United Kingdom and they are of particular use to the Indian government with its aim of controlling manufacturing industry. A review of the detailed disclosure requirements for the profit and loss account in India showed that in certain areas they exceed the United Kingdom requirements.

Apart from financial information companies may disclose social and non-financial information. Social responsibility accounting is an area that is currently attracting attention from academics and practitioners. The extent of social accounting in India was reviewed and compared with the United Kingdom. The use of a value-added statement has become fairly popular in the United Kingdom and a few companies in India have adopted it although distribution of revenue statements are more popular. In the area of employment information the Indian legal requirements stress extensive disclosure of details of higher paid employees. The use of detailed employment reports has not become common in either country although many companies give some items of relevant information in their annual reports. It was found that many Indian companies are providing some social information in their accounts. Information on a wide variety of different items was found. Social accounting is not highly developed in the United Kingdom and it was not clear whether there was much influence on Indian reporting practices in this area.

The final part of this study consisted of a survey of a sample of thirty annual reports of large Indian companies. A disclosure index score was calculated for each company and a mean was calculated for the sample. The level of disclosure of information in India was compared with that in the United Kingdom. It was found that the mean index score for Indian companies was similar to that scored by a sample of fifteen United Kingdom companies in the late 1960s. United Kingdom companies today were expected to score substantially more due to the various developments in financial reporting that have occurred. In support of this contention it was calculated that a company complying with present day legal, professional and stock exchange requirements in the United Kingdom would score substantially higher marks than the average Indian company. The disclosure in the United Kingdom and India was compared on an item by item basis using the results of the surveys of the Institute of Chartered Accountants in England and Wales (1983 and 1984) and the author's survey. Where dissimilar levels of disclosure were observed in the two countries, calculation of the 'chi-square' statistic was employed to determine whether the observed differences were statistically significant. It was found that where Indian disclosure exceeds that in the United Kingdom, this was mainly due to more stringent legal requirements. Where United Kingdom disclosure exceeded that in India the main reason was the existence of an accounting standard in excess of legal requirements.

The level of disclosure was compared not only with the United Kingdom but also with the minimum legal requirements. Indian companies were found to be giving more information than that strictly required by the law.

In conclusion it can be said that financial reporting in India is influenced by regulation and practice in the United Kingdom. The company law relating to financial accounting was originally based on the British model and has since developed to meet the needs of the Indian environment. The Indian accountancy profession has been influenced by developments in the United Kingdom. The accounting standards programme is similar although it is not yet as far advanced. In time the Indian accounting standards will become obligatory as in the United Kingdom and the differences in disclosure in these areas will probably narrow. Other influences may also affect future developments. The United Kingdom is part of the European Community and this will affect the accounting environment. India is a less developed country and future developments in financial reporting may well be affected more by local matters than historical ties and influences.

Appendix A

PROFESSIONAL PUBLICATIONS

Chartered Accountants Act, 1949 (1981 ed.)
Chartered Accountants Regulations, 1964 (1983 ed.)
Professional Ethics : Short Notes on High Court Decisions (1981 ed.)
Professional Conduct : Notes for the Guidance of Members
Code of Conduct (1980 ed.)
Statement on Auditing Practices (1977 ed.)
Statement on the Treatment of Retirement Gratuity in Accounts (1978 ed.)
A Study on Share Valuation (1978 ed.)
Study on Expenditure during Construction Period (1978 ed.)
A Guide to Audit of Public Trusts under the Income Tax Act (1980 ed.)
History of Accountancy Profession in India
Integrated System of Cost and Financial Accounts (1973 ed.)
Organisation of a Chartered Accountant's Office (1976 ed.)
Payment of Bonus Act (1978 ed.)
Audit of Banks (1978 ed.)
Management Control System (1977 ed.)
Statement on the Amendments to Schedule VI to the Companies Act, 1956 (1976 ed.)
Guidance Note on section 293(A) of the Companies Act and the Auditor
Statement on Accounting for Foreign Currency Translation (1976 ed.)
Compendium of Notes (1976 ed.)
Internal Control Questionnaire (1976 ed.)
Monograph on Compulsory Maintenance of Accounts (1978 ed.)
Taxation of Charitable Trusts and Institutions (1980 ed.)
Guidance Note on Additional Emoluments Compulsory

Deposits Scheme, 1974 (1976 ed.)
Statement on Payments to Auditors for other Services (1975 ed.)
Guide to Cost Audit (1981 ed.)
Statement on the Manufacturing and other Companies (Auditor's Report) Order, 1975 (issued under section 227(4A) of the Companies Act, 1956) (1977 ed.)
Information Regarding Registration of Articled and Audit Clerks (1977 ed.)
Technical Guide to Cost Audit Cement Factories (1975 ed.)
Technical Guide to Audit of Sugar Industries (1975 ed.)
Guidance Note on Co-ordination between the Internal Auditors and Statutory Auditors (1979 ed.)
Guidance Note on Accounting Treatment of Interest on Deferred Payments (1979 ed.)
Guidance Note on Accounting Treatment for Excise Duty (1979 ed.)
Training Guide for Articled Trainees (1979 ed.)
Guide to Tax Audit (1981 ed.)
Technical Guide for Audit of Educational Institution (1979 ed.)
Technical Guide for Audit of Co-operative Societies (1979 ed.)
A Guide to Company Audit (1980 ed.)
Taxation of Non-residents (1981 ed.)
Monograph on Accounting for Poultry Farming (1981 ed.)
Statement on Qualification in Auditor's Report (1981 ed.)
An Approach to Social Cost-benefit Analysis under Indian Conditions (1981 ed.)
The Chartered Accountant and Societies
Precedents in Published Accounts (1981 ed.)
Guidance Note on Accounting for Capital Based Grants (1981 ed.)
Compendium of Opinions (1982 ed.)
Accounting and Auditing Technical Guide on Textile Industries (1982 ed.)
Guidance Note on Issue of Bonus Shares
Guidance Note on Accountants Report on Profit Forecasts and/or Financial Forecasts
Guidance Note on Treatment of Reserve created on Revaluation of Fixed Assets
Guidelines on Internal Audit : Jute Industry
Guidance Note on Accounting for Changing Prices

Appendix B

LIST OF ACCOUNTING STANDARDS AND EXPOSURE DRAFTS OF THE INDIAN ACCOUNTING STANDARDS BOARD

Preface to Statement of Accounting Standards

AS1 Disclosure of Accounting Policies
AS2 Valuation of Inventories
AS3 Changes in Financial Position
AS4 Contingencies and Events Occurring after the Balance Sheet Date
AS5 Prior Period and Extraordinary Item and Changes in Accounting Policies
AS6 Depreciation Accounting

ED7 Proposed Statement Accounting for Construction Contracts

LIST OF CURRENT EXPOSURE DRAFTS OF GUIDANCE NOTES

Exposure Draft : Accounting Treatment of Reserves in Amalgamations or Mergers

Appendix C

RESEARCH PUBLICATIONS OF THE INSTITUTE OF COST AND WORKS ACCOUNTANTS OF INDIA

Decisional Phenomena and the Management Accountant
The Break-even Concept and its Practical Dimensions
Financing Asset Replacement
Inflation Accounting as a Tool to Fight Inflation
Inflation Accounting : Tools and Techniques
Management Accounting Problems in Small-scale Industries
Glossary of Management Accounting Terms
Corporate Capital Structure and Cost of Capital
Cost and Quality Control
Monthly Financial Reports for Operating Managers
Cost Accounting in Commercial Banking Industry
Farm Management Accounting and Control

Appendix D

INDEX OF DISCLOSURE

COMPANY NAME DATE

Item of Information	Index Score: Subelement Maximum	Index Score: Total Maximum
Financial History		
10 or more years	(4.00)	
5 to 9 years	(3.00)	
2 to 4 years	(2.00)	4.00
Segment Reporting: Product line		
Sales	2.50	
Operating results	1.50	4.00
Segment Reporting: Geographical area		
Sales	2.5	
Operating results	1.5	4.00
Capital Expenditure: Current		
No details	(3.00)	
At least two categories	(4.00)	4.00
Capital Expenditure: Planned		
No details	(3.00)	
At least two categories	(3.50)	3.50
Depreciation Method	N/A	3.50
Funds Flow Statement	N/A	3.50
Retained Earnings Statement	N/A	3.50

Appendix D

Item of Information	Index Score	
	Subelement Maximum	Total Maximum
Fixed Asset Composition	N/A	3.00
Inventory Composition	N/A	3.00
Price-level Adjusted Statements	N/A	3.00
Market Value of Marketable Securities	N/A	2.50
Currency Translation Method	N/A	3.50
Depreciation Life	N/A	3.00
Foreign Exchange Gains and Losses		
Disclosure if and how foreign exchange gains and losses are reflected in the income statement	N/A	3.00
Sales and Gross Margin		
Sales or gross margin only	(1.5)	
Both	(3.0)	3.00
Income Tax Disclosure		
Disclosure of income tax applicable to current period	N/A	2.50
		56.50

Appendix E

LIST OF COMPANIES INCLUDED IN SURVEY

Name	Date of Accounts
Ashok Leyland Limited	31.12.82
Associated Cement Company Limited	31.07.83
Bata India Limited	31.12.82
Bharat Earth Movers Limited	31.03.82
Binny Limited	30.06.83
Ceat Tyres of India Limited 15 months to	31.03.83
Crompton Greaves Limited	30.06.83
Dunlop India Limited	31.12.82
Godfrey Phillips India Limited	31.12.82
Gujarat State Fertilisers Company Limited	31.12.82
Hindustan Ferodo Limited	31.12.82
Hindustan Motors Limited	31.03.83
Indal Aluminium Company Limited	31.12.82
Indian Airlines	31.03.82
The Indian Cable Company Limited	31.03.83
Indian Farmers Fertiliser Co-operative Limited	30.06.82
The Indian Tube Company Limited	31.03.83
Jagatjit Cotton Textile Mills Limited	30.04.83
Larsen and Toubro Limited	30.09.82
National Organic Chemical Industries Limited	31.12.82
Peico Electronics and Electricals Limited (Philips)	30.06.82
Shaw Wallace and Company Limited	31.12.82
The State Trading Corporation of India Limited	31.03.83
Straw Products Limited	31.12.82
The Tata Engineering and Locomotive Company Limited	31.03.83
The Tata Iron and Steel Company Limited	31.03.83
The Tata Oil Mills Company Limited	31.03.83
Union Carbide India Limited	25.12.82
The Vazir Sultan Tobacco Company Limited	30.09.82
Voltas Limited	30.06.82

Appendix F

COMPANIES IN ORDER OF RANKING BY INDEX SCORES

Name	Index Score
The State Trading Corporation of India Limited	83.2%
Gujarat State Fertilisers Company Limited	80.5%
Indian Farmers Fertiliser Co-operative Limited	78.8%
Indian Airlines	75.9%
Indal Aluminium Company Limited	70.8%
Bharat Earth Movers Limited	70.4%
The Indian Tube Company Limited	68.1%
Dunlop India Limited	67.3%
Ashok Leyland Limited	65.5%
Associated Cement Company Limited	65.5%
Straw Products Limited	63.7%
Ceat Tyres of India Limited	62.8%
The Tata Iron and Steel Company Limited	61.9%
Crompton Greaves Limited	61.1%
Godfrey Phillips India Limited	61.1%
Larsen and Toubro Limited	61.1%
National Organic Chemical Industries Limited	60.2%
Shaw Wallace and Company Limited	60.2%
The Tata Engineering and Locomotive Company Limited	59.3%
The Tata Oil Mills Company Limited	59.3%
Peico Electronics and Electricals Limited (Philips)	58.4%
The Indian Cable Company Limited	57.5%
Hindustan Ferodo Limited	57.4%
Bata India Limited	53.1%
Union Carbide India Limited	53.1%
Voltas Limited	53.1%
Binny Limited	51.3%
Hindustan Motors Limited	51.3%
Jagatjit Cotton Textile Mills Limited	50.4%
The Vazir Sultan Tobacco Company Limited	49.6%

Appendix G

UNITED KINGDOM COMPANIES INCLUDED IN THE 1982/83 SURVEY OF PUBLISHED ACCOUNTS (a) DISCLOSING 'ITEMS OF INFORMATION' (b)

Item of Information	No. of Companies Disclosing	%	Notes[c]
Financial History			
10 or more years	91	30	Table 15.3 shows 6-9
5 to 9 years	18	6	years 18
2 to 4 years	181	60	5 years or less 181
	290	96	No historical summary 10
Segment Reporting : Product Line			
Sales	212	71	Table 18.1 indicates
Operating results	199	66	classification 'usually based on products or services'

Appendix G (cont'd)

Item of Information	No. of Companies Disclosing	%	Notes(c)
Segment Reporting : Geographical Area			
Sales	229	76	Table 18. shows 190 companies disclosed turnover and/or results between countries or continents. 39 disclosed turnover and/or results between the United Kingdom and overseas
Operating results			
No overseas operations	48	16	
Capital Expenditure : Current			Survey does not include this item but fixed asset additions are a requirement of the Companies Act and no audit reports were qualified for non-compliance with this requirement
No details	-	-	
At least two categories	300	100	
Capital Expenditure : Planned			It is a legal requirement to disclose capital commitments and capital expenditure approved by the board but not yet contracted for. No audit
No details	300	100	
At least two categories	-	-	

Appendix G (cont'd)

Item of Information	No. of Companies Disclosing	%	Notes[c]
			reports were qualified for non-compliance with this requirement. There were no quantified statements of future prospects which could have included investment projects (p. 152)
Depreciation Method	282	94	Page 62
Funds Flow Statement	299	100	Table 21.1
Retained Earnings Statement	232	77	Table 15.7 indicates 232 companies classified reserves. No audit reports were qualified in respect of non-compliance with the requirement to show movements on reserves
Fixed Asset Composition	300	100	Table 10.1

Appendix G (cont'd)

Item of Information	No. of Companies Disclosing	%	Notes[c]
Inventory Composition	225	75	Table 22.1
(No stocks shown	3	1)	
		76	
Price-level Adjusted Statements	284	95	Table 6.1
Market Value of Marketable Securities	173	98	Table 15.1
No listed investments	123		
Currency Translation Method	259	86	Table 11.1
Depreciation Life	286	95	Table 7.1
Foreign Exchange Gains and Losses Disclosure of if and how foreign exchange gains and losses are reflected in the income statement	192	64	Table 11.3. 192 companies showed exchange differences in the profit and loss account or in both reserves and the profit and loss account. In addition 54 companies showed exchange differences only in movements in reserves

Appendix G (cont'd)

Item of Information	No. of Companies Disclosing	%	Notes[c]
Sales and Gross Margin			All companies disclosed turnover as this is a legal requirement and there were no qualified audit reports for this reason. No information was given as to disclosure of gross margin
Sales or gross margin only	300	100	
Both	-	-	
Income Tax Disclosure			SSAP8 requires the corporation tax based on the profits for the year to be disclosed. No auditors' reports were qualified in respect of this
Disclosure of income tax applicable to current period	300	100	

(a) 'Financial Reporting 1982-83. A survey of UK Published Accounts' published by the Institute of Chartered Accountants in England and Wales. A survey of the financial statements of 300 listed companies mostly taken from the top 500 of 'The Times 1000 largest UK Companies' accounts issued during the year to 30 June 1982.

(b) Items of information included in 'Financial Reporting Practices : Disclosure and comprehensiveness in an international setting' by Barrett as

Appendix G (cont'd)

categories of information which might be included in a firm's annual report and which could be used as a measure of the extent and quality of financial disclosure.

(c) Table and page number references are in 'Financial Reporting 1982-83'.

Appendix H

UNITED KINGDOM COMPANIES INCLUDED IN THE 1983/84 SURVEY OF PUBLISHED ACCOUNTS (a) DISCLOSING 'ITEMS OF INFORMATION' (b)

Item of Information	No. of Companies Disclosing	%	Notes (c)
Financial History	-	-	Not covered by 1983/84 survey
Segment Reporting : Product Line			Table 2 p. 142. Figures
Sales	205	68[82]	in brackets indicate %
Operating results	190	63[76]	disclosing out of the 250
No disclosure	50	17	companies giving some segmental data
Segment Reporting : Geographical Area			Table 2 p. 142. Figures
Sales	191	64[76]	in brackets indicate %
Operating results	133	44[53]	disclosing out of the 250

Appendix H (cont'd)

Item of Information	No. of Companies Disclosing	%	Notes(c)
No disclosure	50	17	companies giving some segmental data
Capital Expenditure : Current	300	100	Survey does not include this item but fixed assets additions are a requirement of the Companies Act and no audit reports were qualified for non-compliance with this requirement
No details	-	-	
Capital Expenditure : Planned			It is a legal requirement to disclose capital commitments and capital expenditure approved by the board but not yet contracted for
No details	300	100	
At least two categories	-	-	
Depreciation Method	282	94	Page 58
Funds Flow Statement	-	-	Not covered by 1983/84 survey

Appendix H (cont'd)

Item of Information	No. of Companies Disclosing	%	Notes(c)
Retained Earnings Statement	-	-	Not covered by 1983/84 survey
Fixed Asset Composition	300	100	Table 1 p. 52
Inventory Composition	-	-	Not covered by 1983/84 survey
Price-level Adjusted Statements	284	95	Table 5 p. 30
Market Value of Marketable Securities	-	-	Not covered by 1983/84 survey
Currency Translation Method	252	84	Table 1 p. 68
Depreciation Life	285	95	Table 7 p. 58
Foreign Exchange Gains and Losses Disclosure of if and how foreign exchange gains and losses are reflected in the income statement	234	78	Table 1 p. 68
[No evidence of foreign operations	39	13]	
Sales and Gross Margin Sales or gross margin only	300	100	All companies disclosed turnover as this is a

Appendix H (cont'd)

Item of Information	No. of Companies Disclosing	%	Notes[c]
Both	-	-	legal requirement. 'The great majority of the financial statements which are the basis for this edition have been drawn up under the "old" Schedule 8 to the 1948 Companies Act' (p. 1). In future years gross margin will be disclosed if companies adopt the 'operational' profit and loss account format as prescribed by the Companies Act 1981
Income Tax Disclosure			
Disclosure of income tax applicable to current period	300	100	SSAP8 requires the corporation tax based on the profits for the year to be disclosed

(a) 'Financial Reporting 1983-84. A survey of UK Published Accounts' published by the Institute of Chartered Accountants in England and Wales. A survey of the financial statements of 100 large listed, 150 medium listed and 50 large unlisted companies all taken from the top 750 of 'The Times 1000 largest UK

Appendix H (cont'd)

Companies' accounts issued during the year to 30 June 1983.

(b) Items of information included in 'Financial Reporting Practices : Disclosure and comprehensiveness in an international setting' by Barrett as categories of information which might be included in a firm's annual report and which could be used as a measure of the extent and quality of financial disclosure.

(c) Table and page number references are in 'Financial Reporting 1983-84'.

Appendix I

COMPARISON OF % OF COMPANIES DISCLOSING ITEMS OF INFORMATION

Item of Information	Note	India %	UK 82/83 %	Note	UK 83/84 %
Financial History	[1]				
10 or more years		63	30		-
5 to 9 years		23	6 [6-9 years]		
2 to 4 years		13	60 [5 or less]		
Segment Reporting : Product Line					
Sales	[1]	100	71	[1]	68
Operating results	[1]	7	66	[1]	63
Segment Reporting : Geographical Area			No direct comparison possible		
Sales					
Operating results					

Appendix I (cont'd)

Item of Information	Note	India %	UK 82/83 %	Note	UK 83/84 %
Capital Expenditure : Current					
At least two categories	[2]	100	100	[2]	100
Capital Expenditure : Planned					
No details	[2]	97	100	[2]	100
At least two categories		3	Indian companies only diclose capital commitments. UK companies disclose commitments and planned expenditure authorised by the board		
Depreciation Method	[1]	50	94	[1]	94
Funds Flow Statement	[1]	40	100		-
Retained Earnings Statement	[1]	100	77		-
Fixed Assets Composition	[2]	100	100	[2]	100
Inventory Composition	[1]	100	75		-
Price-level Adjusted Statements	[1]	0	95	[1]	95
Market Value of Marketable Securities	[2]	100	98		-

Appendix I (cont'd)

Item of Information	Note	India %	UK 82/83 %	Note	UK 83/84 %
Currency Translation Method	[1]	30	86	[1]	84
Depreciation Life	[1]	3	95	[1]	95
Foreign Exchange Gains and Losses					
Disclosure of if and how foreign exchange gains and losses are reflected in the income statement	[1]	27	64	[1]	78
Sales and Gross Margin					
Sales only	[1]	-	100	[1]	100
Both		100	-		-
Income Tax Disclosure					
Disclosure of income tax applicable to current period	[2]	97	100	[2]	100
Sample size		30	300		300

[1] Calculation of the 'chi-square' statistic indicates that the difference between the two populations India & United Kingdom is statistically significant at the 0.005 level.

[2] Calculation of the 'chi-square' statistic does not provide a reliable result for these observations. However the level of disclosure is clearly basically the same in these cases.

Appendix J

NUMBER OF INDIAN COMPANIES DISCLOSING

Item of Information	No. of Companies Disclosing	%	Notes
Financial History			Legal requirements to
10 or more years	19	63	to provide one year's
5 to 9 years	7	23	comparative figures.
2 to 4 years	4	13	
	30		
Segment Reporting : Product Line			Legal requirement to
Sales	30	100	report sales by product
Operating results	2	7	line
Segment Reporting : Geographical Area			Legal requirement to
Sales	2	7	report total exports

Appendix J (cont'd)

Item of Information	No. of Companies Disclosing	%	Notes
(Exports only	28)	93	
Operating results	0		
Capital Expenditure : Current			Legal requirement to show capital expenditure in categories
No details	0		
At least two categories	30	100	
Capital Expenditure : Planned			Legal requirement to show outstanding contractual commitments for capital expenditure not provided in the accounts
No details	0		
At least two categories	1	3	
Some incomplete information	3	10	
Contractual commitments only	26	87	
	30		
Depreciation Method			
Full disclosure	15	50	
Reference to Companies Act	2	7	
No disclosure	13	43	
	30		
Funds Flow Statement	12	40	
Retained Earnings Statement	30	100	Legal requirement to show breakdown of, and movements on, reserves

Appendix J (cont'd)

Item of Information	No. of Companies Disclosing	%	Notes
Fixed Assets Composition	30	100	Legal requirement to show composition of fixed assets
Inventory Composition	30	100	Legal requirement to show composition of inventory
Price-level Adjusted Statements	0	0	
Market Value of Marketable Securities	26	87	Legal requirement to show market value of marketable securities
Not applicable	4	13	
	30		
Currency Translation Method	9	30	
Depreciation Life			
Full disclosure	1	3	
Partial disclosure	8	27	
No disclosure	21	70	
	30		
Foreign Exchange Gains and Losses			
Disclosure of if and how foreign exchange gains and losses are reflected in the income statement	8	27	

Appendix J (cont'd)

Item of Information	No. of Companies Disclosing	%	Notes
Sales and Gross Margin	30	100	Legal requirement to show sales and gross margin
Income Tax Disclosure Disclosure of income tax applicable to current period	29	97	Legal requirement to show income tax applicable to current period

References

Abu-Jbarah, H.M. (1972) 'A Subentity Basis for Financial Reporting by Multi-national Firms : A Cluster Analysis Approach', unpublished Ph.D. dissertation, University of Wisconsin

Arpan, J.S. and Radebaugh, L.H. (1981) International Accounting and Multi-national Enterprises, Warren, Gorham and Lamont

Barrett, M. Edgar (1976) 'Financial Reporting Practices : Disclosure and Comprehensiveness in an International Setting', Journal of Accounting Research (Spring)

Bhandari, S.K.R. (1973) writing in Indian Manager, Vol. IV, 7

Bose, M. (1977) 'The Growth of Accountancy in India', Accountancy (May)

Bose, M. (1982) 'Wanted : Chartered Accountant Bridegrooms', Accountancy (April)

Brealey, R. and Myers, S. (1981) Principles of Corporate Finance, McGraw-Hill International

Buzby, S.L. (1974) 'Selected Items of Information and their Disclosure in Annual Reports', Accounting Review (July)

Caplan, B. (1983) 'India opts for Liberalisation', The Banker (February)

Cerf, A.R. (1981) Corporate Reporting and Investment Decision, University of California Press

Chattopadhyay, P. (1981) in Enthoven, A.J.H. Accounting Education in Third World Development, North Holland

Choi, F.D.S. and Mueller, G.G. (1978) An Introduction to Multi-national Accounting, Prentice-Hall

Das Gupta, N. (1977) Financial Reporting in India, Sultan Chand & Sons, New Delhi

Emery, D. (1983) 'Industrialisation in India', Barclays Bank Review (August)

References

Enthoven, A.J.H. (1977) Accountancy Systems in Third World Economies, North Holland

Flower, J. (1985) 'Foreign Currency Translation' in C.W. Nobes and R.H. Parker (eds.), Comparative International Accounting, Philip Allan

Gupta, U.L. (1972) Working of Stock Exchanges in India, Thomson, New Delhi

Handa, K.L. (1980) 'Budget Management Techniques : A Perspective for India', Indian Journal of Public Administration, p. 649

Khan, M.Y. (1978) New Issue and Market Finance for Industry in India, Allied Publishers Private Limited, New Delhi

McComb, D. (1979) 'The International Harmonisation of Accounting : A Cultural Dimension', International Journal of Accounting : Education and Research (Spring)

Mehta, B.S. (1980) 'A Disciplined Accounting Profession : Towards Greater Independence', The Chartered Accountant (India) (February)

Mueller, G.G. (1967) International Accounting, MacMillan, New York

Nair, R.D. and Frank, W.G. (1980) 'The Impact of Disclosure and Measurement Practices on International Accounting Classifications', Accounting Review (July)

Nobes, C.W. (1983) 'A Judgemental International Classification of Financial Reporting Practices', Journal of Business Finance and Accounting (Spring)

Nobes, C.W. (1985) 'Depreciation : Can a New Standard Clear the Way?', Accountancy, (March)

Nobes, C.W. and Matatko, J. (1980) 'Classification of National Systems of Financial Accounting', AUTA Review (Autumn)

Pandey, R.K. (1981) 'Delhi's Emergence as a Capital Market', Commerce (October 31)

Price-Waterhouse (1973, 1975, 1979) Accounting Principles and Reporting Practices, Price-Waterhouse in 1973 and 1975, Butterworths in 1979

Ram, M. and Patri, R. (1980) 'Which Way Now for the New Rajahs?', Far Eastern Economic Review (October 3)

Research Committee of the Institute of Chartered Accountants of India (1981) Precedents in Published Accounts, The Institute of Chartered Accountants of India

Sen Gupta, A.K. (1976) Inflation Accounting in India, Research Study of School of Accountancy and Mathematics Calcutta, Finance Publications, Calcutta

References

Sharma, J.L. and Kennedy, R.E. (1977) 'A Comparative Analysis of Stock Price Behaviour on the Bombay, London and New York Stock Exchanges', _Journal of Financial and Quantitative Analysis_, (September)

Singhvi, S. (1967) _Corporate Disclosure Through Annual Reports in the USA and India_, doctoral dissertation, Graduate School of Business, Columbia University

Singhvi, S. and Desai, H.B. (1971) 'An Empirical Analysis of the Quality of Corporate Financial Disclosure', _Accounting Review_ (January)

Zeff, S.A. (1971) _Forging Accounting Principles in Five Countries_, Stipes Publishing Company

INDEX

For Product Safety Concerns and Information please contact our EU
representative GPSR@taylorandfrancis.com
Taylor & Francis Verlag GmbH, Kaufingerstraße 24, 80331 München, Germany

www.ingramcontent.com/pod-product-compliance
Ingram Content Group UK Ltd.
Pitfield, Milton Keynes, MK11 3LW, UK
UKHW020206200926
475702UK00004B/635